PSALM-PRAYERS FOR EVERY MOOD

For Tim, Tony, Frances and Jim

Kevin Lyon

Psalm-Prayers
for Every Mood

the columba press

First edition published, 1996, by
the columba press
55A Stillorgan Industrial Park, Blackrock, Co Dublin, Ireland
This new revised edition published 2000

Reprinted 2005

Cover and typography by Bill Bolger
Origination by The Columba Press
Printed in Ireland by Colour Books Ltd, Dublin

ISBN 1 85607 300 9

Foreword

Nowhere is the soul so bared before God as in the Psalms. They represent the personal struggles and joys of the faithful as they pray out loud to the Lord. These reflection will vividly touch the heartstrings of their readers experiences. The reflections journey from the bewilderment of 'Why us Lord?', to trust and hope even in the depths of suffering and almost despair. We are skilfully brought through the stages of crying out in anger to tranquil acceptance and even joy through an awareness that we are hand in hand with God on our journey. 'Lord must I still struggle on ... yet, Lord, in my confusion I shall continue to trust in your ever present love'. (PS 13)

These reflections blend the psalms with quotations from other parts of Sacred Scripture and the occasional gem from literature. Psalm 96, which urges us to sing out loud in praise of the sheer beauty, wonder and unity of the Lord's creation, 'Let all creation be in harmony', is skilfully grafted to William Congreve's 'music has charms to soothe a savage beast'. Psalm 98, in prompting us to hope, matches Alexander Pope's, 'Hope springs eternal in the human breast' with 'The Lord, the fount of all hopefulness'.

Psalm-Prayers for Every Mood has a thought for everyone and a reflection for every circumstance. Most of all, it encourages us all to take up the psalms and launch into our own conversation where God will speak to the receptive heart. It is a book to dip into by the fireside, in the chapel, on a quiet walk, it can be taken up at any time.

We owe so much to Father Kevin for generously and courageously sharing his faith, experience and thoughts which witness to his enthusiasm and love of the psalms. Taste and eat and share these reflections with your friends.

✠ *Eamonn Walsh*
TITULAR BISHOP OF ELMHAM & AUXILIARY BISHOP OF DUBLIN

Preface

My affection for the psalms dates from the days of Fr Frey's *My Daily Psalm Book* in seminary years of the 50s. These beautiful but sometimes obscure prayers intrigued me. Their very Semitic tone differed so much from the formal pious prayers of the prayer manuals. Above all, these 150 prayer-songs from the Old or First Testament are the inspired word of God, fashioning as it were his very thoughts – the perfect prayer. The psalms were the prayers of Jesus and his mother and later those of the apostles and the first Christians. Jesus prayed the psalms from the cross; they formed his daily communion with the heavenly Father. They encompass the full gamut of yearnings of every Christian: joy and sorrow, the need for guidance, help in times of sickness, consolation in times of trial. In fact, all human life finds an echo in these timeless invocations. Only the Missal can surpass the Book of Psalms in dignity and scope, and the Missal draws heavily upon the psalter.

This is not a translation of the Psalms, nor indeed is it an attempt to summarise them; (some very familiar ones have been left in the original); they are just insights, fleshed out in a world of technology and computers, a 'flash upon that inward eye'. If they should encourage a desire to study and pray the psalms as found in the Bible, then this labour of love will have served its purpose.

How to use this book

The pages of *Psalm Prayers for Every Mood* can be opened anywhere. Or one could consult the Index of Subjects (p 173) and choose a theme that suits the mood of the hour. Read the brief theme in italics, opposite the Psalm Prayer, and then read the text itself at a moderate pace. Re-read the summary and slowly and prayerfully re-read the whole prayer. Sometimes only one Psalm Prayer is sufficient for the occasion, especially as a final adieu to the Lord before settling down for a night's repose.

Kevin Lyon

Reflection from Psalm NO 1

Life is studded with choice – some entail major decisions, others are of lesser moment. Here the Psalmist outlines our options.

THE TWO WAYS

They who choose to lead a meaningful life,
Accept no signals from the indifferent,
They do not conform to the crowd,
Express no prejudices, nor do they
Take satisfaction from the failure of others.

Their ultimate concern is God's will,
Their daily decisions follow his law.

Such a life may be likened to
A sturdy tree, planted in rich loam,
That yields fruit in due season.
Such a soul brings blessings to others.

Not so for those who live without God,
They are like chaff the wind sweeps away, or,
Leaves scattered by an autumn gale;
Empty and fickle, they cannot withstand the word of the Lord.

The children of God walk in his ways,
The children of unbelief thread a dangerous course.

　'Choose here and now whom you will worship
　… But I and my family, we will worship the Lord.' JOSH 24:15

Glory be …

Reflection From Psalm NO 2

We are living in an increasingly secularist society where the material and tangible is all that matters. Here an earthly king offers his crown to the Messiah in token of his submission. This psalm encourages us to trust beyond 'How blessed are all who take refuge in him'. (v 12)

THE MESSIAH KING

Why do the nations stand fast in collusion
In oppressing the people of God?
Why do their followers cherish vain dreams?

Set against each other on many issues,
They are at one in their struggle
To cast off the constraints of belief.

Our God laughs at their senseless endeavours.
One day he will make known to them
Who truly is the Lord and
The King he has anointed.

Even in the midst of my alarm,
He speaks as a loving Father. He says:

'Place your trust in me;
The destiny of the world is in your hands.
You shall overcome one day;
You shall frustrate all attempts
to destroy you.'

Be wise, you who hold high office.
Minister to the God you are trying to stifle.
Bend your heads in meekness,
Do not brave the Lord's anger.

Learn your lesson, you who rule the nations.
Only those who rest in God's will
Are really secure.

'Happy are all who take refuge in him.' PS 2:12

Glory be ...

Reflection From Psalm NO 3

TRUST IN GOD UNDER STRESS

This is a morning prayer of thanksgiving and confidence after a night of repose in the midst of danger. The Psalmist bids us trust God in future conflicts.

Lord, the problems that beset me daily are many.
My dependence on you,
My simple faith in your loving way,
Is constantly under pressure.

And yet, Lord, you are the shield that protects me.
Encircled by your love,
You enfold me with concern,
Your strength supports me.

Past experience has assured me,
That as often as I cried our for help,
My prayer found audience.
Now, I reach out, once more,
You are close to me,
You hear and respond.

Awake or asleep,
I am not troubled by the disputes I encounter.
The conflicts in my life will never separate me from you.

For you are able to salvage
All that imperils my friendship with you.
In your own good time, Lord,
You will set me free.

'Salvation is of the Lord;
your blessing be upon your people!' PS 3:9

Glory be ….

Reflection From Psalm NO 4

All the good that is in us, is from God. We can be confident that what God has bestowed he will not suffer to be lost. Sleep is his blessing for the night, just as peace is his blessing during the day.

A NIGHT PRAYER

When I call on your name, O Lord,
You give ear to the sound of my voice.
Now let your face shine upon me.

In the troubles of the past,
You took note of my affliction.
Swiftly you brought me relief.
Have pity on me now, hear my prayer.

Whatever of worth lies within,
Has come from your bounteous hands,
Do not now allow, what you bestowed to perish!

Remind me constantly,
That I truly belong to the Lord;
That he feels for me when I suffer.
O foolish heart of mine, calm down,
Renew your reliance on God.

You are the only good.
Our hearts are destined
To rest in you alone
Driving out fear,
Restoring our peace.
Reveal to us the sunshine of your favour.

A sigh is heard,
From a people who yearn for the light of better days.
They cry out: "Who will show us good things?"

And yet, I have come across more joy
In my companionship with you,
Than in rich possessions.

Even as I lie down, sleep comes gently,
And with sleep, tranquillity.
With the Lord on my side,
I am never alone.

'As soon as I lie down, I fall asleep in peace,
for you alone, O Lord, will keep me safe.' PS 4:9

Glory be ...

Reflection From Psalm NO 5

'AT DAWN YOU HEAR MY VOICE'

Lord, lend an ear to my words,
Listen to the voice of my pleading.
Be our strength every morning,
Facing the sacrament of your presence,
My King and my God.

Lord, the world fashioned by your hands,
Seems to be in chaos, in disarray.
Men and women living only for themselves,
Imagine you are not essential to them.

Yet, of myself I know well, that,
I cannot be devoted to your service,
Without the assurance of your abiding love.

Help me to walk today in your path for my life,
Grant me the strength to overcome
The many barriers on the road.

The conditions on this planet
Bear scant resemblance to your truth.
Subtle and seductive voices incline us to stray.
Enable us, Lord, to recognise them for what they are:
Shallow, superficial, ultimately unwholesome.

Those who follow your way need have no fears,
Continually you unveil yourself to them.
You care for them with compassion,
Basically their plans are your own.

  'The Eternal God is you dwelling place,
  And underneath are the everlasting arms.' DEUT 33:27

Glory be ...

About to offer the morning sacrifice, the Psalmist feels his own unworthiness before God and asks that his prayer for integrity be heard, as he bows down towards the Temple in reverence.
'Then I looked up and saw the morning rays, mantle its shoulder from the planet bright, which guides our feet aright on all their ways.'
— DANTE ALIGHIERI

[14]

Reflection From Psalm NO 6

RECOVERY FROM AN ILLNESS

Lord, when you reprove me,
Let it not be in anger.
When you chastise me,
Let it not be in displeasure.

But the truth is
I am feeling poorly,
Wretched, and with little strength left,
I am in deep distress.

I beg you, Lord,
Relieve me from this gnawing pain.
Weary with my moaning, I cry out in the night..
The agony I endure, will it ever end?
O Lord, how long …?

Heal me! I am trembling with apprehension.
Reassure me once more of your love for me.
Rescue me for your mercy's sake.

Graciously, the Lord heard my pleading;
I implored and my prayer won acceptance..

   'The Sun of justice will arise
   With healing in his wings.' MAL 4:2

Glory be …

All the Old Testament writers looked upon suffering as a result and punishment for sin, and to a certain extent they were right. Jesus, in the ninth chapter of St John's Gospel corrected the notion that suffering and affliction are the result of personal sin.

Reflection From Psalm NO 7

Most of us need the encouragement and incentive that comes from some positive achievement, some real good that we are able to do.

THE ENEMY WITHIN

O Lord, I hasten towards you like a trembling fugitive.
Save me, protect me, from all who stalk me,
Like beasts of prey.

Should I be held accountable for their hostility,
Paying back evil,
A destructive influence in society,
Then, level my pride with the dust!

But you know well, Lord, the inner recesses of the heart,
Those base cravings that lurk in unruly flesh.
You know too, that in spite of good intentions,
The most subtle foe of all is myself.
How cowardly I am in conforming to my finer instincts.

Yet, you have pledged to me your protection.
No thought or desire of mine escapes your scrutiny.
You have determined my sinfulness;
Now Lord, set me free from its sinister consequences.

Will there ever be an end to evil?
When will this thwarting tussle cease?
Strengthen me towards some lasting good,
To win the sunshine of your smile.

Well known the end of those who thrive on evil.
Their malice recoils on themselves,
Their violence will fall on their own heads.
Shelter me from jealousy that I may feel kindly towards all.

I take refuge in the Lord in my brokenness,
That I may walk in his strength towards the prize.

Glory be ...

Reflection From Psalm NO 8

God's majesty is manifest in creation. Yet, he has allocated a dignified role for us humans. Here the Psalmist contrasts the might of the universe with the exalted role of humankind.

A COSMIC HYMN

O Lord, our Master,
How the majesty of your name fills all the earth!
Your greatness overflows the heavens.
I observe the images of your craftsmanship
And the sound of your glory at every approach.

The work of your fingers,
The moon to mark our calendar, and,
On the parchment of the heavens,
You imprint the signature of your stars.
Even the chuckle of babes and the laughter of children
Spell out your name in so many ways.
'I look around and the world is full of God.'
What then is Adam's breed that it should claim your care?

I ponder in amazement my Creator's involvement with me,
That he cares about me,
Moulding me in his image,
Placing me only a little below the angels.

The glory and honour which gleam from the human soul,
Outshines all other reflections of your majesty,
In the depths of the sparkling heavens
You have fashioned humankind
As finite lord of the universe!

You, Lord, have given us faculties
To hear and understand you.
Sharing with us your creative activity,
You give us power over the work of your hands.

'God our God, how glorious is your name over all the earth!' PS 8:9

Glory be …

Reflection From Psalm NO 9

THANKSGIVING AFTER VICTORY

I will give thanks to you, O Lord, with all my heart:
I will sing praise to my God, the Most High.

You helped me to stand-up to those,
Who tried to vilify me.
They simply faded away.

Great evils take root from small beginnings,
They spread like a pestilence.
But integrity and noble character
Rise from simple acts, affirmed,
They climb to the highest heaven.

You, Lord, overthrew the great armies in history,
They pitted their might to oppose you.
The monuments to tyrants,
Now crumble in the dust.

You remained on to rule our broken world,
That those born of earth strike terror no more.
Your strong arm extended to the oppressed
Your compassion towards those afflicted by war.

You know well my own fears and doubts.
So often you held me back from the brink.
I tried to alleviate the misery of others,
Then I found relief in my own distress.

Ungodly nations sink in their own misery,
They are caught up in their own deadly devices.
The patience of the afflicted will not go for nothing,
You heed them, and bring courage to their hearts.

  'Lord, I give you all the thanks of my heart.' PS 9:1

Glory be …

The Psalmist looks beyond his own needs and troubles to the needs and troubles of others. In this he is a model for us all, and provides one of the best and surest means of relieving our own distress.

Reflection From Psalm NO 10

IS GOD DEAD?

Why, O Lord, do you seem to stand afar?
Why hide in a time of distress?

Reflecting on our world today,
There are those who appear to thrive without you,
While others make themselves the centre
of their own little universe.
Still others, are limited to the carnal.
All are at one in assuming that 'God is dead.'

Yet, these are the ones who look as if they are flourishing
They are distrustful of human goodness.
They ridicule those who show compassion.
Overbearing in their speech,
Haughty in their attitude;
Concern for the poor and marginalised never crosses their minds.
They appropriate what they covet,
Regardless of the hurt they cause.
Arise, O Lord, come to our aid!
You whose eyes are moved to pity,
Innocent or guilty, you read every heart.
Now, says the Lord,
I will bestir myself on behalf of the defenceless
Who are so ill-used;
Of the poor who cry out so bitterly.
I will win them the redress they long for.
Yes, Lord, you will watch over us, and
Keep us safe in these evil days.
You are Lord of the universe.
You hear the prayers of honest folk.

'O Lord, you hear the laments of the poor,
You strengthen their will, you listen to their cry.' PS 10:17

Reflection From Psalm no 11

A Song of Trust in God

Lord, each day bears a fresh load of care.
I am frightened by the insecurities around me.
I am tempted to take refuge in foolish adventures,
Escaping like a scared sparrow to the hillside.

But there is no easy flight from reality.
Even when we rise from our torpor
And return to moderation,
Our follies are still present to confront us.

Look kindly on me, O Lord,
Give ear to my prayer,
Light to these eyes before they are
Closed in death.
You are in our midst,
You are in your holy shrine,
Ever aware of the apprehensions of
Your beloved children.

True, you may not always banish our fears, yet,
You pledge to confront them with us,
Making them stepping-stones of faith,
Drawing us closer to yourself.

I cast myself on your mercy;
Soon may this heart of mine
Boast of redress granted and
Sing in praise of your bounty.

> 'For God is good, and he loves goodness.
> The godly shall see his face.' ps 11:7

Glory be …

Reflection From Psalm NO 12

IN EVIL TIMES

'There is no God above',
Is the fond thought of heedless minds.
'Piety is dead and in a base world, true hearts have grown rare'

They speak falsehood,
With forked tongue and double heart.
They boast of violent deeds while,
Claiming to be seeking peace.

But the Lord will not remain silent forever,
His word is one and firm, eternal and creative.
His voice will drown out
The vaunted pride of the unfaithful.

'The ill-treated and the poor have suffered long enough'
says the Lord. 'I will bestir myself on their behalf
and win them the redress they long for.'

The promises of the Lord are proven metal;
well and truly refined.
His word is one and true and alive and
What he pledges, that he will do.

Preserve us dear Lord,
From ignoble compromise and
The conceited arrogance
Of this generation!

> 'The words of the Lord are pure words,
> like silver refined in an earthen furnace,
> purified seven times.' PS 12:5

Glory be …

Reflection From Psalm NO 13

St John of the Cross wrote extensively on what he first termed 'The dark night of the soul' – a deep sense of dryness in prayer, a time of depression for the faithful soul. Here the Psalmist describes the symptoms and appeals for relief in his darkness.

DARK NIGHT OF THE SOUL

Lord, must I still struggle on, all unremembered?
Sometimes you appear so far away,
Your look turned away from me.

I can no longer sense your presence or feel you,
This blackness about me is suffocating,
The gloom within overwhelms me.
How long more must I harbour sorrow in my soul,
Grief in my heart, day after day?

Enter into this dark night, O God;
Fill-up this immense void.
Break into this bleak cabin.
Give light to my eyes,
Lest I fall asleep in death.

Yet, Lord, in my confusion,
I shall continue to trust
In your ever present love.
Soon to discover once more,
Delight in my friendship with You.

My heart rejoices in your salvation;
I will sing to the Lord,
'He has been good to me!' PS 13:6

> 'The soul's dark cabin, battered and decayed;
> lets in new light through chinks that
> time has made.' – WILLIAM BLAKE

Glory be …

Reflection From Psalm NO 14

Sin brings its own punishment, here and now, and this fact is a deterrent, but it is not enough. The positive help of God is necessary to lead a good life.

GENUINE SERVICE

How senseless are they who would claim that
God is dead!
Who deny the existence of a Supreme Being.
'They eat the bread of God, but do not invoke his name.'
Not even a thought of their Creator,
Their days lived out in godless abandon.

Yet, our great God is ever casting around
For hearts that are open to him.
Their very words, telling of his presence;
Their deeds, fragrant with his gentle touch.

Denial and rebellion were ever the mark of Adam's breed,
Even the good we do remains so often tarnished;
While sin and wickedness dull the soul,
And leave a heart of stone.

We are apt to be more destructive than creative,
Neglecting to place our lives in your keeping.

Yet, the Lord works through the lives
Of those who trust in him,
Earnest folk dedicated to his service.

'Whom shall I send? ... Here I am Lord; send me.' ISAIAH 6:8, 9

Glory be ...

Reflection From Psalm NO 15

Christianity looks to Jesus Christ as the model for perfect behaviour, whose teachings were fulfilled in his own manner of living. He has left us a means by which we can become God-like.

THE MARKS OF FELLOWSHIP

What is required, Lord,
For entry into your house?
What are the conditions
Of belonging to your family?

Surely it is those whose lives are guided by your way,
Who are open and honest in their dealings,
Who speak and act in kindness towards others.
They play no part in schemes that promote injustice;
And come what may, they are always true to their pledged word.

These are the ones
Who are permanently in the Lord's friendship.

  'No one who so acts can ever be shaken' PS 15:5

Glory be …

Reflection From Psalm NO 16

THE GOOD NEIGHBOUR

Keep me safe, O God,
To You have I come for refuge.
I say it again; 'You are my Lord.
I have no other help but yours.'
I thank God,
For the kindness of the people
In this neighbourhood where I live.
I have found their friendship,
A great support and comfort.

He has given me a beautiful portion!
Pleasant brooks and meadows surround me.
He guards all that is mine.
He tells me what to do.

I look to the Lord as my counsellor.
Late into the night
He is ever ready
To teach and guide me.

Is it any wonder I am happy?
I am always thinking of the Lord,
I never need stumble and fall.
Heart, body and soul are filled with joy.

The Lord shows me the path of life,
Fills me with gladness in his presence.

  'You have put into my heart an incredible love
  For the faithful ones who dwell in your land.' PS 16:3

Glory be …

We were made for God, because we have a nature and capacity which only he can fill and satisfy. Creatures are not enough for us, because at best they are but glimpses and faint images of the Almighty.

Reflection From Psalm NO 17

BURN OUT

Lord, I believe I have a just complaint,
Hear my story, don't let me down.
I have always tried to play fair.
Never have I resorted to the physical

I have kept my feet firmly on your paths,
Championed your cause, proclaimed your word.
You have told me of your love
In the words of your Book;
But true love is shown
Not only in words, but in deeds.
Now surprise me with your grace, and
Bless me with your help!
Those I serve don't appear to respond.
They seem indifferent to your word.
I reach out in concern and I am cold-shouldered,
They just don't want to know me.
Lord, I am weary of well-doing,
I feel burnt out.

Now, guard me as the apple of your eye.
Hide me in the shelter of your care.
Encourage me in the work I am doing,
That inner peace,you alone can bring.
I know that one day, I shall see your face,
And be filled with the sight of your glory.

  'Guard me as the apple of your eye.
  Hide me in the shadow of your wings
  As you fly over me.' PS 17:8

Glory be ...

Reflection From Psalm NO 18

If we count our own blessings and reflect on some of the misfortunes we have escaped, we shall always have much to thank God for as well as praying for other poor mortals who have been less favoured than we have been.

CONTENTMENT

Lord, you have removed from my life
The fear of death.
What follows the grave no longer terrifies me.
The agonising happenings of this life,
May worry me, but can never crush me.

You are my rescuer, my niche of refuge,
To you I run for safety.
You have given me your salvation as my shield,
Your gentleness has made me great.

What a God he is!
Earthquakes, volcanoes,
Even the lightning that encompasses the skies,
The waves that thunder against our shores,
All nature bears witness to his majesty.

The Lord reaches into my busy life.
He surrounds me with eternal love.
He heals my wounds.
He sets me free to serve his creatures.
He shields me from all harm.
Is it any wonder that I love him?

Into my keeping he pours out his gifts
To share with those who are in need.
Entrusting me with tasks too great for me,
He empowers me to bring them to completion.

'In my pain I begged the Lord for help.
And he heard me from his Temple.
My cry reached his ears.' PS 18:6

Glory be …

[27]

Reflection From Psalm NO 19

MORE PRECIOUS THAN GOLD

See how the skies make known the glory of God!
How the vault of heaven declares
His craftsmanship!
Wherever I am, wherever I travel,
I can perceive something
Of the majesty of our God.

The magnificence of the mountains,
The immensity of the oceans,
The fascination of outer space,
All announce the power of God.

Even amid the bustle of our teeming cities,
Are reflections of the work of his hands;
He makes his presence known throughout the universe.

The Lord has made his eternal truths known
From his word, and his law
Printed on the heart of humankind.
These precepts which direct us on the paths of peace.

He has given substance to my life,
Placed before me the goal of this creation.
Fulfilling humanity's greatest needs,
He has answered our deepest yearnings.

All these are more precious than gold,
Sweeter than honey dripping from its comb.

My pilgrim way on this planet
Presents no smooth path.
Plagued by lapses and hidden faults,
I stumble daily.
Yet your love and your grace sustains me.

'May the spoken words of my mouth,
The thoughts of my heart,
win favour in your sight, O Lord,
my rescuer, my rock!' PS 19:14

Glory be …

Reflection From Psalm NO 20

In the original Psalm we have a prayer for victory as the king is about to battle against powerful enemies. The words in the Psalm offered for success in the conflict are adapted here to form the outline of a letter sent to a sick friend for recovery.

A LETTER TO A SICK FRIEND

My dear friend,
I hear you are not well,
that illness has confined you to bed.
We pray for your speedy recovery to good health.
Our prayer is this:

'May the Lord listen to you in your time of need.
May the power of God be your protection!
May he send you aid from his holy place.
May he remember all the sacrifices you have made
When you were strong and healthy.
May he grant you your heart's desire
To be up and well again to carry on the good work,
Crown your hopes with fulfilment.
We are all looking forward to the day of your recovery.
Others may talk about wonder drugs
And advances in medical technology,
But our prayer for you is in the name of our God,
the Great Healer.
O Lord, save our friend,
hear us in this our hour when we call on you.'

Adieu.

Reflection From Psalm NO 21

GOD IS WITH US IN TROUBLE

I rejoice in your strength, O Lord
My heart is full of gratitude
Every time you save me.
You have given me my heart's desire.

You have not held back from what I asked.
You welcomed me into your house with many blessings,
Strengthening me with gifts from your altar.
You fulfil the desires of the human heart.

Whatever of value has come from your hands.
My heart is moved by your compassion;
Being with me in sorrow,
Now you rejoice in my victories.

Even when I am attracted by material things,
And base instincts lure me astray from you;
Yet, I am comforted by the smile of your favour.
Your love is steadfast
As the Northern Star.
You are always with me,
Abandonment you know not.

  Stand high above me Lord,
  In your protecting strength;
  'We will write songs to sing
  Of your mighty acts!' PS 21:13

Glory be …

If we who are so frail are disposed to be generous towards those who are truly grateful, how much more will God be inclined to help his children who show thankfulness for his gifts!

Reflection From Psalm NO 22

This is the greatest of the Passion Psalms. The opening words were spoken by Jesus from the Cross. It is a graphic description of our Saviour's crucifixion and agony.

SUFFERING OF THE MESSIAH
(The ideal prayer for all who suffer)

My God, my God, why have you deserted me?
You are far from my plea and the cry of my distress.
O my God, I call by day and you give no reply;
I call by night and I find no peace.

You are nonetheless, dwelling in the holy place;
It was in you that our fathers trusted;
They trusted and you set them free.

But I, down and out, have no dignity left,
The butt of the rabble,
The laughing stock of the people.
All who see me deride me;
Mouthing out insults,
While they toss their heads in scorn.

'He trusted in the Lord, let him save him:
Let him release him if this is his friend.'
I was cast upon you from my very birth;
From my mother's womb you have been my God.
Be not far from me, for trouble is near
And there is none to help.

Many foes, like bulls have surrounded me
And hedged me in.
Against me they opened their mouths wide,
Like a lion roaring for its prey.

I am spent like spilt water,
My bones disjointed,
My heart like molten wax within me.

My strength is dried up,
Like clay in the baking.
With thirst my tongue sticks fast in my mouth.
You have laid me in the dust to die.

Prowling about me like a pack of dogs,
Their wicked conspiracy hedges me in;
They have torn holes in my hands and feet;
I can count my bones, one by one; and
They stand there watching me,
Gazing at me in scorn.

They divide my spoils among them,
Cast lots for my garments.
Then, Lord, do not stand at a distance,
Look to my defence.
Only one life is left me;
Save me from the sword,
From the power of these dogs;
Rescue me from the very mouth of the lion,
From the horns of the wild oxen
They have brought me so low.

Glory be …

Reflection From Psalm NO 23

The most beautiful of shepherd songs describes God's loving care for the Psalmist.

I SHALL NOT WANT

The Lord is my shepherd; I shall not want.
He gives me a resting place where there is green pasture,
Leads me out by still waters,
And revives my drooping spirits.

By sure paths he leads me;
He is true to his name.

If I should walk in the valley of darkness,
I will fear no evil.
Your rod and your staff;
With these you give me comfort.
Envious my foes watch,
While you spread a banquet for me.

My head you have anointed with oil;
My cup is overflowing.

All my life long, your loving kindness pursues me;
In the Lord's house shall I dwell forever and ever.

Glory be …

Reflection From Psalm NO 24

The pious Hebrew loved and revered the Ark of the Covenant because it was the symbol of the special presence of God on earth. The Ark was a figure and a type of the Christian tabernacle, where Our Lord dwells as our eucharistic God.

PRAYER BEFORE A LITURGICAL CELEBRATION

The earth belongs to the Lord!
Everything in all the world is his!

Who then may serve the Lord in truth?
Who may go to the place where he lives?
Who may stand before the Lord?

Surely it is the men and women
Who are aware of the God's designs,
Whose hands are clean and hearts pure.
Their deeds untainted by falsehood,
Who open wide the door of their hearts?

These are the ones who are allowed to stand before the Lord.

'Fling wide the gates, open the ancient doors,
and the Holy One will come in!' PS 24:9

Glory be ...

Reflection From Psalm NO 25

REPENTANCE

All my heart goes out to you,
Don't fail me, Lord, for I am trusting you.
After the degradation of defeat
I look to you for kindness and support.

Don't let my sinfulness triumph,
My failures gain the victory over me.
Bring light to the darkness in my heart,
Some reason for my very being.

Have you kept a record of my misdeeds?
Then overlook my youthful sins,
How many they are!
Oh, forgive them for the honour of your name.

Look upon my emptiness and loneliness,
Consider kindly my afflictions and despair.
Remember the never ending presence,
Of human fragility, unwholesome passion.

Relieve this heart of mine of its burden,
Deliver me from my distress.
Look kindly in judgement on my sin,
My grevious sin.

O Lord of mercy,
I realise my guilt is great,
Heal those who humbly reach out to you.
See my sorrows.
Feel my pain.
Forgive my sins.
Restore me to yourself.

Our proneness to wrongdoing, as well as our endless needs, creates an ever present necessity of appealing for help and pardon to our Heavenly Father who has revealed Himself as a God of love and mercy.

Watch over me
Lest I fall again.

'Remember, O Lord, your mercy and faithful love,
For they are from the beginning of the world.' PS 25:6

Glory be …

Reflection From Psalm NO 26

The Psalmist is conscious of his own integrity, and therefore concludes with confident hope that, with God's guidance in decision making, his prayer is heard.

DECISION

O Lord, I have loved the beauty of your house,
This place where the brightness of your presence lives.
I have trusted you without turning back.
I come before your altar singing a song of thanks.

Always your mercy dwells in my thoughts,
Your faithfulness is ever at my side.
My prayers like incense rise before you.
I wash my hands to prove my innocence.

Now, today, Lord, the moment of decision has arrived.
Guide my steps as the road before me is so uncertain.
There are dangers en route as
Tempting allurements beckon me off course.

Help me to take the right fork on the road to life;
Your finger-postings ever directing me aright.
Then I will stand on firm ground where his people gather.
I will join in blessing the Lord's name.

'For the day of the Lord is near in the valley of decision.' JOEL 3:14

Glory be ...

Reflection From Psalm NO 27

LIGHT AND SALVATION

The Lord is my light and my salvation,
He protects me from danger.
So whom shall I fear?

The baseness of this world cannot overcome him,
Nor can it crush anyone within his care.
The business of this fast moving life,
May threaten my peace and serenity,
But, with the Lord on my side,
I shall gain the mastery.

One request I make to the Lord,
For this I long.
To be accepted as a loyal member of his kingdom, there
To experience his affirming touch,
To behold his beauty
To contemplate his Tabernacle.
For he says, 'Come and talk with me ,
O my people,' and my heart responds,
'Lord, I am coming.'

The Lord is my light and my salvation,
Even should my own relatives turn from me,
Yet will he welcome and comfort me.

'Don't be impatient.
Wait for the Lord.
He will come and save you!
Be brave and take courage!
Yes, wait and he will help you.' PS 27:14

   'I shall light a candle of understanding in your heart,
    Which shall not be put out.'   2 ESDRAS 14:25

Glory be …

Reflection From Psalm NO 28

The Psalmist pleads earnestly that his prayer be heard and that he be saved from sharing the fate of evil-doers. He concludes that the Lord will protect and bless him.

MY ROCK OF SAFETY

O Lord, hear the voice of my pleading,
For you are my Rock of safety, my refuge.
I lift up my hands to heaven
I cry out for your help.

I must mind every step, test every stone.
You are my Pillar of Strength in the firmness of your word,
In the uniqueness of your truth,
By the permanence of your eternity.

Do not number me among the hypocrites
Before the throne of judgement,
Those who talk peace to their neighbours,
While mischief is in their hearts.

You are my Rock, my Crag, my Prominence,
In the midst of waves, above the storms.
Only to look at you calms my soul, bestows peace.
I lean against your might, safe and secure.

'Oh, praise the Lord!
He is my strength from every danger.' PS 28:6-7

Glory be ...

Reflection From Psalm NO 29

The power and the majesty of God as revealed in a thunderstorm is the theme of this Psalm. The Lord who, through the phenomena of nature is reflected as mighty and terrible, can and will give security and peace to his people.

NATURE SPEAKS OF GOD

Give to the Lord
The glory due to his name.

The majesty of God is manifest in his creation;
The voice of the Lord echoes from the clouds,
The skies and the emerald forests, are
All the beauty of his crafting.

The utterance of the Lord resounds over the waters,
His echo thundering in the swollen rivers,
Out of the raging flood he makes his dwelling place.
His voice topples the cedars of Lebanon,
Sets the oak trees a-swaying,
Strips the deep forest bare.

Even the accomplishments of human hands
Transpire by way of his wisdom;
Meadows ripe for the harvest,
The harnessing of our waterways,
The founding of great establishments.
Do these not also reflect the work of his fingers?

 'And this Lord will give strength to his people;
 the Lord will give his people his own blessing of peace.' PS 29:11

Glory be …

Reflection From Psalm NO 30

We have here a song of thanksgiving for deliverance from what threatened to be a fatal illness. The Psalmist has been snatched from the very jaws of death. He gives praise and thanks to the God who loves to show mercy.

DELIVERANCE

I will praise you, Lord!
You have rescued me.
I cried to you for help.
You brought me back from the brink,
I give thanks to his holy name.

Then in my prosperity I said,
'This is forever. Nothing can stop me now!
The Lord has shown me his favour
He has made me steady like a mountain.'

But, just as thick clouds obscure the sun,
So, was the face of my God.
You cut off from me your river of blessings.
I felt empty and unfulfilled.
I was at peace no more.

I cried to you, O Lord, I asked,
'How can I tell about your fidelity?
How could dust in the grave speak out?
Oh, have pity and help me.'

It was then that the Lord,
Turned my anguish into gladness.
He took away my clothes of mourning.
Sorrow was but the guest of the night,
But joy came in the morning.

  'O Lord my God, I will keep on thanking you forever.' PS 30:12

Glory be ...

Reflection from Psalm NO 31

The Psalmist is in great distress; but recalling past favours and mercies is emboldened to pray and hope for relief.

'MY LIFE IS IN YOUR HANDS'

Lord, I have passed through tough times.
The props that I thought would sustain me,
Have been knocked from beneath me:
I have collapsed like a tent unpegged.

Now my health is broken from sorrow.
I have become weak from grief,
My years drained away in sadness.
I feel like a broken crock.

Now there is nowhere else to go,
Nothing to cling to,
No foothold to balance,
My faltering steps.

I recall that in past times,
You took pity on my weakness.
You took note of my affliction,
Heeded my soul's distress.

Be now a cave of refuge for me,
A mighty stronghold to save me.
For your name's sake,
I will rejoice and be glad of your kindness.

I look only for your guidance,
My fate is in your hand.

   'Cheer up! Be brave!
   Take courage if you trust in the Lord.' PS 31:24

Glory be …

Reflection from Psalm NO 32

Psychologists and spiritual guides of many creeds have long realised the healing balm of confession of sin as a road towards reconciliation with God and neighbour.
'We must not daydream tomorrow's judgement – God must be allowed to surprise us.'
– PATRICK KAVANAGH

BEFORE RECONCILIATION

What happiness for those whose guilt has been
    forgiven!
What joy when transgressions are buried deep!
What relief for those who have confessed their
    sins!
What peace when God has cleared their record!

As a mother loves and pities
The weak child of her womb,
So does the Lord who made us,
Love and pity each child of Adam.

There was a time when I wouldn't admit what a sinner I was.
I kept my sins secret, ignoring them, rationalising them.
Not telling the truth only made me sad.
My strength was dried up, as though parched by a summer's heat.
But now, I have acknowledged my sins.
My guilt I did not hide.
I long to be transparent to myself and to you.
I will be my own accuser and say:
'I will confess my offence to the Lord.'
And you forgave me!
All my guilt is gone.

  'Don't be like a senseless horse or mule
    That needs a bit in its mouth to keep it in line!' PS 32:9

Glory be …

Reflection from Psalm NO 33

The same God who created the universe has a master-plan for all creation. This Psalm moves us to celebrate that great design in songs of praise and thanks-giving.

THE PLANS OF THE LORD

How good it is to sing a hymn to our God,
How delightful to praise our Glorious One.
Celebrate with the old songs of applause,
Compose new songs, that tell of his eternal love.

The Creator frustrates the plans of the nations.
He sets their objectives at naught.
He holds back his hand from destruction,
From the face of the earth.

His own plan stands forever.
His purposes are the same for every generation.
He has made their hearts.
Happy that nation whose God is the Lord,
The people he has chosen as his patrimony.

It was the Lord's word that made the heavens,
The breath of his lips that peopled the earth.
He spoke, and they were made,
He gave his command and they were fashioned.
He delivers his children from the fear of death,
And through them gives life to this planet.

'Yes, Lord, your plans stand forever,
the thoughts of your heart to all generations.' PS 33:11

Glory be …

Reflection from Psalm NO 34

*All human senses
respond to God.
Here the Psalmist
invites the prayerful
to taste and see that
there is meaning
and purpose in the
midst of suffering.*

TASTE AND SEE

The praise of the Lord is always on my lips.
Come and rejoice with me,
For he is ever gracious and kind,
All who are discouraged take heart!

I cried out to the Lord in my anguish
And he responded.
I shed tears in vexation
Over the hassle I went through,
But he was near me, my firm support.

What the Lord has accomplished for me,
He can fulfil in you.
He is close to the broken-hearted.
Those whose spirits are crushed he will save.

Enter into his presence,
He will fill your emptiness with abundance,
Strengthen your weakness with his power.

Taste and prove it; the Lord is good.
He is very near to those who suffer,
He reaches out to rescue
Those battered down by despair.

'Why do the faithful ones have to suffer?'
The anxious query of innocent souls.

'Taste and see that the Lord is good.
They are happy who seek refuge in him.' PS 34:9

Glory be ...

Reflection From Psalm NO 35

Few of us can live happily without affirmation, acknowledgement, approval of our life's role. We need some kind of recognition. This Psalm explores this seal of approval.

'I AM YOUR SALVATION'

To follow your way Lord, is a daily challenge.
I stumble along well-worn paths.
Buffeted by strong winds, I grope in the darkness.

Have I not earnestly tried
To relate to those around me?
Attempting to reach out in loving concern,
Sharing their joys and sorrows?

Yet, the heartening response I craved, eluded me.
I felt used, discarded,
Like a sucked orange on the scrapheap of life.
Save me from those who wish me ill.

We are but instruments in your hands, O Lord,
Conduits through which your goodness flows.
Remove all bitterness from my heart,
Make me kind and gentle, so they return the favour!
Save me from the blight of jealousy.
I must not give up, Lord,
Even though the going is tough.
I feel tired. I fall many times.

I need desperately your touch of joy,
Your affirmation as I struggle on.

O Lord say to my soul; 'I am your salvation.'
'Courage, my dear friend,
I realise well, you are under pressure.
I am with you all your days,' says the Lord.

Glory be …

Reflection from Psalm NO 36

Here the Psalmist prays that his Eternal Benefactor may ever continue to show him favour and protection. The Lord is his fountain of life and the closer he is to him, the more replete he is with life.

THE FOUNTAIN OF LIFE

Lord, your mercy reaches to the heavens,
Your faithfulness,is expansive as the billowing
    clouds.
Your justice stands firm as the everlasting hills;
The wisdom of your decrees, like the fathomless depths.

How precious is your kindness O God!
Under the shelter of your canopy
The frail children of earth find confidence.
To both humans and animals you give protection.

From the rich store of your house you will nourish them,
They slake their thirst at the fountain of contentment.

  'For you are the fountain of life.
  Our light is from your light.' PS 36:9

Glory be …

[48]

Reflection from Psalm NO 37

We must not expect
God to do for us
what we can and
should do for
ourselves.

WAIT FOR THE LORD

Are you impatient friend,
At the apparent prosperity of the wicked?
Do you envy those who thrive on evil,
Enjoying success at every turn?

Then, remember that the mercies of the Lord
Are above all his works.
Trust in him, do your best,
He will grant your heart's desire.

Be kind and do good to others.
Then you will live safely here in the land.
You will succeed in all you do,
Trust him to help you do it, and he will,
Making your integrity as clear as the morning light.

So, calm your anger,
Overlook the rage within.
Do not fret,
It might only lead to evil.
Be patient, it will take time,
Let your serenity confirm your peace;
The victory is ultimately the Lord's.

> 'Be still before the Lord, and wait patiently;
> Do not brood over those who prosper on their way,
> over those who succeed by devious means.' PS 37:7

Glory be …

Reflection from Psalm NO 38

It is difficult for people who have never been afflicted by depression to empathise with those who are cast down and see only a bleak future. This psalm helps us to understand in some measure, the plight of the depressed.

THE APPEAL OF A SINNER

Lord, there are many evils in this world.
My weak nature inclines me powerfully
Towards the very misdeeds
That bring about my deepest woes.

I am sick with sin and failure,
My head is reeling,
My whole body is aching.
I have lost my appetite.
I get no sleep.
I have no desire to see anyone, or
Be seen, in my hour of misery.

Those I once called my friends,
Now stay their distance.
I have lost contact with old companions.

Now I am silent as one who cannot speak.
I have nothing to say,
For I am waiting for you,
O Lord my God.

You are aware of my anguish, Lord.
You feel my misery.
I am ever ready to publish my guilt,
Ever anxious over my sins.

O Lord, my God, do not forsake me!
Listen to my defence.

  'Help me, O my Saviour!' PS 38:22

Glory be …

Reflection from Psalm NO 39

Here the Psalmist reminds us power-fully of our brief life-span on this planet. Only works of enduring value will count in the end.

THE BREVITY OF LIFE

Lord, I have tried to bear the pain in silence.
Alas! No satisfaction in repressed indignation.
Now I can be silent no longer.

Lord, warn me of my end.
How brief are the days in this span of life.
Their very brevity brings home to me how frail I am.
'As soon as we were born, we began to draw to our end.' WIS 5:13
My lifetime is as nothing in your sight.

Only a breath is any human existence,
A mere shadow without any lasting substance.
All our busy rushing around ends in nothing.
Even the goods we accumulate, who's shall they be?

And now, Lord, what is there to wait for?
In you rests all my hope,
Set me free from my sins.

Unravel these random thoughts of mine.
Don't sit back, not seeing my tears.
I am a traveller passing through this earth,
A pilgrim, just as my fathers before me.

   'Your life, what is it?
   You are no more than a mist,
   Seen for a little while and then dispersing.' JAMES 4:14

Glory be …

Reflection from Psalm NO 40

No sooner has one petition been answered than other pressing needs call for attention. This Psalm is a prayer of thanksgiving and petition for continued help.

A NEW SONG TO SING!

I waited patiently for the Lord to help me.
Then he listened and heard my cry.
He freed me from a quagmire,
He set my feet on a hard, firm path.
He steadied me as I walked along.

He has given me a new song to sing.
He has put meaning and gladness into my life.
Now, I will go to others and invite them,
To put God back into their lives.
Those who are disillusioned
By life's fleeting delights,
Will also have something to sing about.

The real sacrifice you long for
is that of lifelong service.
I feel so happy doing what you want,
For your law is written in my heart.

Meanwhile my sins have all caught up with me.
They are now too many to number.
I feel ashamed of my weakness and infidelity,
But consoled that,
'My name has been written on the palm of his hand.' IS 49:16

The Lord smiles on all who love him.
May they constantly say,
'How great God is.'

Glory be …

Reflection from Psalm NO 41

A significant feature of our day is the proliferation of caring agencies for third world countries. Here the Psalmist in a global sweep outlines the motivation that lies behind enterprise.

CONCERN FOR THE POOR

Blessed are those whose thoughts of concern
Are with the poor and the marginalised.
They are the happy ones in your Kingdom.

Thank you Lord for the gift of awareness
Of injustice and oppression,
To the awakening to liberation,
In the structures of society;
To denounce poverty and to oppose tyranny.

You have moved our thinkers to think, and
Our people of action to act.
You have opened our eyes to see in the poor
Our suffering brothers and sisters.

They are our members in pain,
Together with us,
Of the one body
Of which you are the Head.

As all are equal in the love you bestow,
So, may all be equal in the use of the goods
You have freely made available,
To all your children.

   'Happy those who help the poor and the lowly.'
   God will help them when they are in trouble.' PS 41:1

Glory be …

Reflection from Psalm NOS 42-43

Men and women know that they have within themselves a ceaseless craving for satisfaction and completion which they do not and cannot find on earth. It is this great 'something' we call God.

THIRST FOR GOD

Like the deer that pants for running streams,
So my soul is yearning for you my God.
I thirst for God the living God.
Where can I find him to come and stand before
      him?

Now I long for a deeper sense of your presence.
To meet you in prayer, in the stillness of my heart,
To relish once more those treasured moments,
Anticipating heaven on earth.

I recall so well, that lively faith of my youth,
How I sang so vibrantly those hymns of praise,
How I listened intently to your word
Ever eager to join family and friends
In the house of the Lord.

But now, my heart feels empty.
Doubt like a wave floods my soul.
I try to pray, but there's a dryness within.
Even the very though of heaven seems hollow.
I hear voices around me say;
'Where is your God?'

O Lord, send forth your light and your truth
Let them lead me to your Holy Place.
There I will go to the altar of God.
I will go with great joy.

  'He will make me smile again.
  For he is my God.' PS 43:5

Glory be ...

[54]

Reflection from Psalm NO 44

An urgent need to be free from present distress, reminds the Psalmist of God's past mercies. This gives him confidence to persevere in prayer.

PAST GLORY AND PRESENT NEED

Lord, how I love to recall past times!
How you were so close to your people.
The ways they defeated their opponents,
And attributed their success to you.

It was not the instruments of war,
Or valour on the field of battle,
That won the day.
They conquered because
You smiled on them and loved them.

My constant boast is the Lord,
I can never thank him enough.

But for sometime now I miss your intimate companionship
Of former days.
Have you left the scene?
Tossed me aside?

Now I am in deep trouble.
I have no one but you to turn to.
No better than sheep marked down for slaughter.
Had I forgotten the name of my God in prayer,
Or allowed my heart to become entangled;
You, who know what is in me,
Would have found me out.

But I have not forgotten you, Lord,
I worshipped and sang your praises,
When all was well.
I dedicated myself to your service.

Do not now hide your face,
Or forget my need in distress.

Deliver me from this cut and thrust
Before it is too late.

  'Arise, Lord, and help me in your mercy,
  Claim me as your very own!' PS 5:4

Glory be …

Reflection from Psalm NO 45

Every one needs at least one close friend. Here the Psalmist expresses that joy of friendship where God is also a partner.

GRATITUDE FOR A FRIEND

My heart is full of joy today. I feel great!
As I search for words to express that gladness,
Volumes tumble from my lips.

You, my beloved, were the source of delight.
You affected me by your kindness.
You made it good for me to be alive.

I glimpsed the beauty of God in his creation.
He was present in eyes that looked lovingly on me.
He reached out through your glance of concern.
He put new meaning in my life; kindled a fire within.

You, my dear friend, showed me a better way,
You took away my confusion;
Put order and meaning
Into my aimless strivings.

Gratitude is now the theme of my song.
Now I pray that the Lord may use me,
As he has so graciously used you;
To give joy where there was sadness,
Hope when near to despair.

May the Lord keep us both safe in his keeping.
May he make us messengers of tranquility;
Your loving kindness to me, always remembered.

Reflection from Psalm NO 46

BE STILL!

God is our refuge and our strength.
He is a sure help in days of trouble.
Even when the world seems to dissolve in chaos, and
Nations are wracked by wars;
Yet, I will never doubt that our Great King is with us.
He has come to save us.

He counsels me, 'Wait quietly, and you shall have proof
        that I am God.'
Hurry blinds me to your presence.
Feverish activity allows no time for you.
Only in the peace of my soul do I recognise you.
Only in the silence of my heart can I worship you.

Soothe my emotions;
Heal my anxiety;
Allay my fears.

  'Be still! and know that I am God.'
  He is our refuge and our strength. PS 46:10

Glory be ...

Reflection from Psalm NO 47

The Psalmist calls upon all nations to unite with him and his people in shouting God's praises to the skies and accepting his worldwide dominion.

THE VICTORIOUS KING

Come, everyone, and clap your hands for joy!
Sing triumphant praises to our God.
For the Lord is tremendous beyond words.
He is the mighty King of all creation.

He rules the nations with fairness.
Rich are the blessings he lavishes on his people.
From the abundance of his storehouse,
He provides for the nations.

God has gone up with a mighty shout.
He has ascended with trumpets blaring.
Sing out your praise to our God.
For he is King of all the earth.

'My soul overflows with praise to the Giver of all good things.'
PS 47:7

Glory be …

Reflection from Psalm NO 48

THE PRESENCE OF THE LORD WITHIN

How wonderful is our God!
High above us puny mortals,
He soars above the plains for all to see.

Only the Lord can satisfy
The vast capacity of the human soul.
He sweetens the barren wastelands
With his presence.
Reaching out with compassion,
He draws us to himself.

The strength of the Holy City
Is not in her bulwarks and stones,
But in the presence of the Lord within.
Within the City's walls,
God has proved himself a sure defence.

Pass it on to the next generation.

'O God, we ponder your love within your temple.
Your praise, O God, like your name
reaches the ends of the earth.' PS 48:10-11

Glory be …

Experience has taught us that the presence of one very dear, can make tolerable even a bleak environment; whereas the richest surroundings can become cold and desolate when a cherished spirit has departed.

Reflection from Psalm NO 49

The worldly rich cannot take with them their wealth. In the grave their riches cannot help, is the theme of this Psalm as it explores the riddle of life.

THE RIDDLE OF LIFE

How foolish those who hoard wealth!
How feeble those who trust in their own strength,
And boast of great possessions.
Matched with the brute beasts,
They are no better.

Material opulence may prolong the span of human life,
It can never purchase exemption from the grave.
The rich and the poor,
The high and the low,
The strong and the weak;
All must return to the dust.

The longest earthly life is but a passing breath.
Weighed up with the aeons that preceded it,
Or the eternity to follow,
It is beyond compare.

What good to strut and fret one hour upon the stage,
Bow out to plaudits and be seen no more?

How brief the fleeting days of life!
How vain that wealth that cannot
Buy off the reaper, death!
In the clay of earth,
Their riches cannot help them.

Establish in your life the eternal joy
Of knowing and relating to the Lord.
You need not then depend on this world's wealth,
Nor fear the end of your days.

From the sleep of death,
You will wake to everlasting enjoyment;

From the darkness of the grave
Come into eternal morning light.

　'The Lord will ransom you from death
　And take your soul to himself.' PS 49:15

Glory be …

Reflection from Psalm NO 50

A timely reminder of the true worship of the heart which the Lord requires and which alone avails for salvation.

THE ACCEPTABLE SACRIFICE

Lord, you are present on planet earth.
Your boundaries stretch from East to West.
Your duration lasts from dawn to dawn.
You are the King of all creation.

The Lord speaks to the citizens of the world.
He speaks to them gently in love.
He is ever mindful of the frailty of humankind.
He judges his people with fairness.

He addresses those who are faithful to his word.
He reassures them and challenges them.
He affirms them and commissions them.
His message is this:
'My friends,
Remember well these words of mine. The offerings you make to me are only externals, mere drapery for what is unseen. You realise that I already own the gifts you bring. After all it was I who brought them into being. Nor is there any need to erect memorials on my behalf. All creation is testimony to the work of my hands. The real sacrifice I yearn for is fidelity to that bond of love I have covenanted with my people. Rather offer your gifts on the table of humanity's needs. It is in this way that I touch the lives of the needy. These are the real sacrifices I desire, and without them, no other gifts would be pleasing to me.'

   'Is not this the sort of fast that pleases me:
   To break unjust fetters,
   To undo the thongs of the yoke.
   To let the oppressed go free,
   And to break all yokes?' IS 58:6

Glory be …

Reflection from Psalm NO 51

THE PRAYER OF A REPENTANT SINNER

Have mercy on me O God,
As you are ever rich in mercy;
In the abundance of your compassion,
Blot out the record of my misdeeds.

Wash me clean from my guilt,
Purge me of my sin.
The guilt which I freely acknowledge,
The sin which is never lost to my sight.

You only my sins have offended;
It is your will I have disobeyed;
Your sentence was deserved.

For indeed, I was born in sin;
Guilt was with me already
When my mother conceived me.

But you are a lover of faithfulness.
And now, deep in my heart,
Your wisdom has instructed me.

Sprinkle me with a wand of hyssop
And I shall be clean;
Washed, I shall be whiter than snow;
Send me tidings of good news and rejoicing,
And the body that lies in the dust
Shall thrill with pride.

Turn your eyes away from my sins,
Blot out the record of my guilt;
Bring a clean heart
To birth within me;

Breathe new life, true life
Into my being.

Do not banish me from your presence,
Do not take your Holy Spirit
Away from me;
Give me back the comfort
Of your saving power,
Strengthen me in generous resolve.

This tongue shall boast of your mercies;
O Lord, open my lips, and
My mouth shall tell of your praise.

You have no mind for sacrifice,
Burnt offerings, if I brought them,
You would refuse.
The sacrifice God loves
Is a broken spirit;
A heart that is humbled and contrite,
God will never disdain.

Glory be ...

Reflection from Psalm NO 52

Some of us are often
apt to sit content
and to let the rest of
the world, and
especially those
whom we consider
sinners; go their way
to judgement and
punishment. The
true spirit of
Christianity is
otherwise.

THE CHAMPIONS OF INFAMY

There are those in our world today
Who see no need of help from the Lord.
Replacing deceit for integrity,
They are enmeshed in a life of crime.

They lure and then use others,
To advance their evil ways;
Employing them as stepping stones
To boost a bloated life.

Not so with the children of God;
Rich possessions may not be theirs,
Yet will they trust in divine mercy,
A clear conscience being their greatest treasure.

Such are like the fruitful olive tree
In God's garden.
Nourished from its roots,
They will find refreshment in its shade.

   'But I am like a sheltered olive tree.
   I am protected by the Lord himself.' PS 52:10

Glory be ...

Reflection from Psalm NO 53

The really foolish ones of this world are those who bypass God in their lives. Here the Psalmist reviews the state of those who live a godless existence.

THE WORLD WITHOUT GOD

Foolish hearts declare; 'We have no need of God,'
Their thoughts are not raised on high.
Reflection and pursuit of the Lord
Forms no part of their plans.

God looks down from heaven
upon all the human race
to see if there be anyone wise,
anyone who searches for God.

They live out their daily lives,
As if the Almighty never existed.
They have missed the mark
And rebelled against him.

Sin and wickedness, when persisted in,
Dull the mind and harden the heart;
Against the Lord and the realm of the spirit.
Enslaving its victims to this passing world.

> 'The wise of heart will heed the commandments,
> but a prating fool will come to ruin.' PROV 10:8

Glory be …

Reflection from Psalm NO 54

The Psalmist rejoices at the thought that God has a name; he can be called, can be addressed, can enter into dialogue with humankind, and encountered as a person, in confidence and familiarity.

THE POWER OF HIS NAME

Come with great might, O Lord, and save me!
Save me, O God, by the power of your name.
Hear my pleading.
Give ear to the words of my mouth.

I was caught up in a web of my own confusion.
The unkindness I gave vent to was my undoing.
I spoke without reflection.
I behaved badly.
I caused distress to those I love.
I had no thought of God's law to check me.

Ah! But the Lord is always near to help me.
He is a friend of mine!
He touched me with his love.
He set me free to walk in his presence.
I will own up to him with willing heart.

Lord, make me a channel of peace
Towards those I have hurt by my sin.

   'Save me, O God, by the power of your name.' PS 54:1

Glory be ...

Reflection from Psalm NO 55

Life in a modern city can be fraught with tension. This contemporary Psalm pictures the city-dweller caught up in a lonely city. Having been betrayed by a former close friend, he/she decides to struggle on.

THE CITY

I feel lonely, Lord, in this city.
But I know well that I am not alone,
For you are near to guide me.

When I first experienced these cobbled streets,
I fancied that I could cast off
The restraints of my youth;
Taste new freedoms from kith and kin.

Now, that experience has been bitter-sweet.
There is crime in the neighbourhood.
My place was ransacked.
I see strife and violence; blood on the pavement.

I had a friend for company, an intimate friend.
We walked together in harmony to the house of God.
We had wonderful talks late into the night.
With such a friend, life was tolerable.

But now, that friend has turned against me
Avoids contact with me,
Despises me.
Sweet words, but knives underneath.

Oh! for wings like a dove,
To fly away and be at rest.
I would travel to distant places.
There I might find refuge from all this turbulence.

But I will not go away.
I will remain on in this city.
I will endure its scars in my flesh.
I will bear its shame in my soul.

'I will redeem the sufferings of the city I love.' CARLOS G. VALLES

Reflection from Psalm NO 56

Walking is one of the most enjoyable activities in life. The Psalmist walks with God side by side. Supported by the nearness of his presence, he is sustained on the journey through life.

WALK BEFORE THE LORD

O God, it was you who fashioned the world,
Everything within reflects the beauty of your
      wisdom.
You, Lord, possess the fullness of being,
Nothing defective finds its source in you.

But why so much wickedness, Lord.
What evils abound on planet, earth!
Why so much mischief from Adam's breed?
Human hearts might rest satisfied
If they knew the reason why!

You, Lord, would have us understand,
That you alone are perfect.
The evils in this world arise
From the limitations and defects,
Inherent in every created being.

You have kept the answer to our queries
In deep mystery.
Being all-wise, all-perfect, all-powerful,
You have your reasons, Lord,
For permitting it to be so.

Such knowledge is veiled to us now.
We must walk before the Lord in faith.
We cannot depend on sense alone.

The awards that await us for bearing with faith,
And patient trust, are everlasting.

  'Now I can walk before the Lord in the land of the living.' PS 56:13

Glory be …

Reflection from Psalm NO 57

Unwavering trust in God, in the midst of surrounding danger, is the dominant thought of this Psalm.

THE OLD ENEMY

Have mercy on me, O God, have mercy!
Here is a soul who puts its trust in you.
I will take refuge under the shelter
Of your wings, till the disaster passes.

My days are full of care,
I am weary of the demands
That are made upon me,
My spirit bowed down in distress.

I am always afraid
Of losing the battle
To the old enemy within;
My own weaknesses and failures.

But today, Lord,
My heart is quiet and confident;
I like to greet the morning with song!

Show your presence through all I encounter.
I will thank the Lord throughout this day.

'I mean to thank you among the peoples,
To sing your praise among the nations.
For your love reaches to the heavens
And your truth to the skies.' PS 57:10

Glory be ...

Reflection from Psalm NO 58

FALSE SHEPHERDS

Lord, there are some in positions of trust today;
Alien to them is the thought that
You are the source of all authority;
That with you, is the seat
Of final reckoning.

Did they but come to terms with wisdom itself,
How markedly different would their actions be?
Might they not now be so eager
For high office?

As it is, Lord, they strut and preen.
Their actions are defiant of a higher power.
They deal out nothing but oppression.
They play god with the lives of their subjects.

They manipulate others into carrying out their purposes.
Through bribery and corruption,
They spawn their little band
Of loyal followers.
Their rituals are all a sham.
Hypocrisy is their badge of shame.

They are poisonous as deadly snakes.
They are cobras that close their ears
To the most expert of charmers.
O God, break off their fangs!

  'Forbid, O Lord,
  That I should ever turn from you,
  To follow the false shepherds of this world.' CARLOS G. VALLES

Glory be ...

Lord Acton (1834-1902), British historian, once wrote in a letter to Bishop Mandell Creighton; 'Power tends to corrupt and absolute power corrupts absolutely.'

Reflection from Psalm NO 59

THE ONE DISCORDANT NOTE

Lord, you made us.
From the clay of earth you fashioned us.
Man and woman you breathed upon us.
All creation is the work of your hands.

On reflection on the myriad of wonders
Of earth and sky, so pleasing to the eye,
Of vegetable, mineral and animal life;
This world abounds in endless variety.

Yet, from your finest achievement,
Emerges that one discordant note
In the mighty music of creation
The sinfulness of humankind.

How often our joy is turned to sorrow,
Our pleasures into pain,
Our singing into mourning?
Who lives today, returns to dust to morrow.

But, you, Lord, are our tower of solidity.
You are our fastness and our refuge.

'I turn to you, O God my strength,
For you are my stronghold.' PS 59:17

Glory be …

That men and women are capable of sinning is the one discordant note in the whole of God's creation. However, the Lord is our tower of strength and we can implore his assistance, especially in times of trouble.

Reflections from Psalm NO 60

How frequently does our folly lead us into peril and grief! We are led astray by what at best are only shadows of God. To seek the things that are above, requires effort and a strength which only God can provide.

SHADOW AND SUBSTANCE

Lord, how often do our follies menace us?
Bereft of sound judgement we are defenceless,
But, you, Lord, are our strong point.
You are our well trusted friend.

So often we pursue only the shadow of your
        presence.
We see only a dim view of your face.
We follow the trailing clouds of your wisdom.

We search inside ourselves
Only to find the cupboard bare.
We hanker after favour and applause,
We invest resources in things material.

Why, Lord, are we so weak?
Why are we bound so much to earth?
Why do allurements and attractions,
The pleasures of the flesh,
Make so strong an impact?

To be sensual, fleshly, carnal,
Is so easy, Lord; no problem!
While the hallowed and the the blessed,
Need our efforts and
Your healing touch.

In your wisdom, Lord,
You do not force your gifts upon us.
For you, our freedom is paramount.
We make every struggle to follow your way.

Grant, that after chasing the shadows,
We don't miss out on the substance!

Glory be …

Reflection from Psalm NO 61

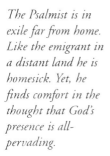

The Psalmist is in exile far from home. Like the emigrant in a distant land he is homesick. Yet, he finds comfort in the thought that God's presence is all-pervading.

PRAYER OF AN EXILE

A deep longing overcasts my soul.
Nostalgia like a garment wraps me round.
Do not let this yearning go unheeded,
Though I call upon you,
From the ends of the earth.

I recall the happy days I spent
Close to your tabernacle, Lord.
Dear though home was to me,
It is more precious to me now,
Exile that I am.

> 'I shall live forever in your tabernacle
> Oh, to be safe under the shelter of your wings!' PS 61:4

Glory be …

Reflection from Psalm NO 62

The Psalmist finds peace and confidence in the thought that God is his salvation and his hope. Compared with the strength of his Lord, all the power of material wealth is as nothing – mere vanity.

GOD IS IN CONTROL

Silently I stand before the Lord.
Salvation comes from him alone.
Safe in his protection,
I fear no deadly fall.

I trust in the Lord completely.
He is all-powerful, all-holy.
His loving glance watches over me.
From the cradle to the grave he is concerned.

Why then do so many not trust in him?
With twisted words and honeyed tongues,
They try to undermine our deepest convictions;
Disturbing the very foundations of our faith.

Why then should I be tense with fear
In time of trouble?
Why be so anxious about future happenings
When success is in the hands of the Lord?

O my people, trust in him at all times.
Tell him what you need, for he can help!
Even the great ones and the lowly
Are as nothing in his sight;
Weighed up, they are less than air on scales.

God has said it many times.
The momentum belongs to him alone.

  'He rewards each one of us
  According to what we deserve.' PS 62:12

Glory be …

Reflection from Psalm NO 63

A TIMELESS THIRST

O God, my God, how I long for you!
How I thirst for you in this dry and weary land,
A land without water.

My soul craves its own perfection.
Its happiness and satisfaction
Rests in you alone, my God.

No created goods can supply all we want.
At best, all earthly belongings are limited.
Accumulated together they
Cannot satisfy our needs.

Satiety leaves a vast void,
Ever yearning for more or
Something else,
But never filled.

Where, Lord, are the clear, clean waters to be found?
So many drink from shallow muddy pools,
Broken cisterns, they
Miss out on the fountain of living waters.
They grope as in the dark,
Seeking, striving, longing;
Yet not knowing which way to go.

Lord, supplement our poor natures,
Support our weak efforts,
Guide us towards the oasis of life-giving waters.

   ' … my heart thirsts for you,
   my body longs for you,
   as a land parched, dreary and waterless.' PS 63:1

Glory be …

Clean, clear water is the number one priority of all healthy living on this planet. So often today it is expensively bottled or difficult to locate. Here the Psalmist contrasts the basic thirst for clean sources of water with his primal need for God.

Reflection from Psalm NO 64

The Psalmist accepts the hurt that comes from the bitter words of others and finds consolation from the word of God in the Scriptures.

ARROWS

Lord, give ear to my cry in my hour of need.
Save me from the guile of base humanity.
From the schemes of the malevolent, deliver me.

They aim their bitter words like arrows;
Silent, pointed, deadly, their sharpened
swiftness strikes; fateful death on the
Winds of hatred.
Suddenly the deed is done.
They meet in secret to set their traps.

Such are the deluded lovers of self.
They lack a sense of natural decency.
Fair play is not their practice.

Why, Lord, should the inoffensive
Suffer from the words of others
Why should their evil seeds grow
To wound humankind's noblest depths?

'Apt words have power to soothe
The tumours of a troubled mind
and are as balm to festered wounds.' JOHN MILTON

The protection you give, Lord, is your word.
Against the arrows of humankind, the arrow of God.
It illumines my mind and steadies my heart.
Your word gives me peace and joy forever.

   'But God shoots them down with arrows
   Their overthrow is sudden.' PS 64:7

Glory be ...

Reflection from Psalm NO 65

Thanksgiving for the fruits of the harvest is as old as the Feast of Tabernacles (The Feast of Ingathering – a harvest festival for the fruits of the threshing floor and the wine-press. It's a feast of rejoicing.) Here the Psalmist in a wide sweep garners the ingredients that encompass his gratitude.

HARVEST THANKSGIVING

Well earned the praise we give you, Lord.
To you we pledge our word, hearer of prayer.
To you all must look for pardon,
Weighed down by sinfulness till you forgive.

Fill our hearts with love of your house.
As we confidently approach with hope,
There in serenity and peace;
We number our blessings.

The more blessed, the more thankful
We should be, Lord.
May we never fail to fully acknowledge your bounty.

You water the land and care for it,
Enriching it with natural resources.
You drench its furrows.
You bless its crops.

You crown the year with your goodness.
The hills are clothed with gladness.
The meadows are covered with flocks.
The valleys are decked with grain.

We are truly grateful, O Lord.

'Thanksgiving the memory of the heart.' ANON

Glory be …

Reflection from Psalm NO 66

AS SILVER IN A FURNACE

Come and see the deeds that God has done.
The marvels he has accomplished among his
      people.
He made a dry road through the sea for them.
They went across on foot.
What joy there was that day!

The era of God's mercies never ceases,
Our destinies he holds in his hands.
He watches every movement of the nations.
He keeps our feet on a sure path.

He has refined us, as silver in a furnace.
In the crucible of suffering he appraises us.
We went through the valley of pain and sorrow.
But in the end, he brought us freedom.

Now, I renew my commitment to the Lord.
He would not have listened if my heart
was set on wrong.
But the Lord heard me.

  'For the Lord did not refuse me his kindness and his love.' PS 66:20

Glory be …

There is a cleansing effect when metal is exposed to great heat. It loses its dross and in this thermal state is often malleable. The Chosen People of the Exodus went through trial and suffering, 'as silver in a furnace', before entry to the Promised Land. Here the Psalmist contrasts the ordeals of former days with the purifying suffering of our day.

Reflection from Psalm NO 67

Here the Psalmist rejoices that the Good News of God's Kingdom is being spread abroad. The hallmark of the authentic message will be revealed in the inner peace it bestows on those who accept the tidings.

A MISSIONARY PSALM

O God, in mercy bless us.
Let your face beam with joy
As you look down on us.
Send us around the world
With your good news for all humanity,
Your saving health among all people.

All nations will learn the truth
By the peace it brings its followers.
How glad those people will be,
They will sing for joy!
The earth continues to receive
The abundance of our God.
This is because you are their king.
And you will give true justice to your subjects.

May every abode,
Every hamlet,
Every village and town,
Every city and suburb;
Echo to the praise of their God!

   How beautiful on the mountains,
   Are the feet of the messenger announcing peace,
   Of the messenger of good news,
   Who proclaims salvation and says to Zion,
   'Your God is king!' IS 52:7

Glory be …

Reflections from Psalm NO 68

The God of the Old or First Testament, and the New is the same. What was veiled so often in the old was revealed in the new.

DOES GOD CHANGE?

Lord, you are ever with your faithful ones.
No one can snatch us from your loving embrace.

The history of your chosen people
Well attests your saving care.
To those who love and serve you,
You are their friend,
Their protector,
Their deliverer,
Their God.

What happened, Lord,
That a life so full of joy and light
Should end in sorrow and deep darkness?
Were not your glowing promises
Made to stand forever?

Did God change?

Like the bright stars, like the sun,
Whose light and warmeth
Continue the same,
Even after storms and clouds
Have shut us away from them,
So, God continues the same.

It is always the sinner who turns away from God,
Who walks out of light into darkness.

Only God can be trusted. He is:
   'Our way, our truth and our life.' JN 14:6

Glory be ...

Reflection from Psalm NO 69

Here we catch glimpses of the future Messiah like sparks of light that illuminate the Psalm. The reader is invited to study the Psalm (PS 69) in a modern translation (NJB/RSV)

A GLIMPSE OF THE FUTURE MESSIAH
'They hated me without cause.' (JN 15:25)

The cleansing of the Temple
'Zeal for Your house will consume me.' (JN 2:17)

His Passion
'A bowl of vinegar stood there; so they put a sponge full of vinegar on hyssop and held it to his mouth.' (JN 19:29, 30)

Reference to Judas
'Let his habitation become desolate, and let there be no one to live in it; and his office let another take.' (ACTS 1:20)

To the Jews who rejected him
... and David says, 'Let their table become a snare and a trap, a pitfall and retribution for them; let their eyes be darkened so that they cannot see, and bend their backs for ever.' (ROM 11:9, 10)

In reference to Christ
... our Christ did not please himself; but as it is written, 'The reproaches of those who reproached you fell on me.' (ROM 15:3)

Reflection from Psalm NO 70

Here the Psalmist seems impatient with God, who is urged to 'rush to help.' His fear is that life will ebb away before he has had an opportunity of straightening things out before the final curtain.

RUSH TO HELP ME

Rescue me O God!
Lord hurry to help me!
Fill your followers with joy.
Let those who love salvation speak up.

Let them say:
'What a wonderful God he is!'
But I am in deep trouble.
Rush to help me
For only you can support and save me.
O Lord, don't wait!

I fear that life will ebb away
Before I accomplish my tasks.

I want to be loyal and true.
For that I require your help,
Your blessing and your grace.

   'But I am in deep trouble.
   Rush to help me.
   For only you can help and save me.
   O Lord, don't wait!' PS 70:5

Glory be …

Reflection from Psalm NO 71

People are now living longer than ever. Most men and women can aspire to reach their 70s and 80s. This implies growing old gracefully. This Psalm should give encouragement to those who are touching the Autumn years of life.

NOW THAT I AM OLD AND GREY

Lord, you are my place of safety,
The home, where I always feel welcome!
You have been in my life
As far as my memory goes back.
I have learned your name from my mother's lips.

Now that I am old and grey,
Don't set me aside.
'The years as they pass
plunder us of one thing after another.' HORACE
Thank you for being with me through my life.
Don't leave me when my strength is failing.

People view me now as a 'survivor',
'Look,' they say,
'Isn't he/she great for his/her years?'
Now, give me grace to age well,
To feel kindly till the end.

I have always told others
Of the great things you do;
Your constant daily care,
How I walked in your strength,
How you saved me from bitter trouble.

Now that I am looking down 'the arches of the years'
'Into the lean and slippered pantaloon' SHAKESPEARE,
Give me time to talk to this new generation,
To tell stories to their children of
The countless, wonderful deeds,
Of your kindness and your love.

You will bring me up from deep in the earth,
You will bring me back to life again,
Give me greater honour than before.

'I will be your God through all your lifetime.
Yes, I will be with you even when your hair is white with age.
I made you and I will care for you.
I will carry you along and will be your Saviour.' ISAIAH 46:4

Glory be ...

Reflection from Psalm no 72

A description of the ideal king, the Messiah, and of his eternal, universal and beneficent reign.

THE KINGDOM OF THE MESSIAH

O God, help the king to judge as you would.
The king's son to walk in integrity.
Help him to give justice to your people,
To show compassion for the weak and the needy.

Let him reign from sea to sea,
Rule to the ends of the earth.
Yes, the leaders of the nations
Will acknowledge his sovereignty.

Such a harvest his people will reap!
Peace on every mountain,
Justice on every hill-side.
All will live in harmony forever.

His people will bless him all day long.
He will help the poor who cry out to him,
They have no one else to defend them.
He will save them from violence,
For their lives are precious to him.

Blessed is his great name forever,
Let the earth be filled with his glory.

'May the reign of this son of mine be gentle and fruitful.' PS 72:6
'Thy kingdom come.'

Glory be …

Reflection from Psalm NO 73

Envy can eat into the heart of the noblest deed. We feel sad when others do well. Here the Psalmist recalls that only lasting contentment can be found in God's evenhanded favour towards all humanity.

THE IMPULSE OF ENVY

Lord, I was envious of those who were rich.
Why should I feel sad when others succeed?
All through life, their path is smooth.
Healthy and trim is the image they project.

They don't have problems like the rest of us.
They have all that money can buy, no problems.
They are carefree, even malicious, disgustingly smug.
Yet, people honour and applaud them.

Meanwhile, God's people are downcast and confused.
'Does the Most High know what's really going on?
Is it to no good purpose that we kept our hearts true?
Why do those who despise your kingdom prosper?'

Then one day, I went into God's sanctuary to think.
I thought about the future of that amoral set.
What a slippery path they are on!
Their bright bubble will burst one day.
Their present life is only a dream.
They will wake up to the truth too late.

You, Lord, are all I ever need,
My constant companion;
You lead me in a way of your own choosing.
Direct me with your wisdom and instruction.

The paltry delights of prosperous worldlings,
Are passing and incomplete at best.
Sweet communion with our God,
Is the alliance that nothing can break.

  'Now guide me with your counsel and
  Receive me into glory at last.' PS 73:24

Glory be ...

[88]

Reflection from Psalm NO 74

Many wars wrack our planet earth. War is a dark blotch on the escutcheon of humanity.

WAR

O God! how many conflicts rage in our world today!
Step carefully through the utter ruins;
Bombed out places of worship,
Hospitals, pock-marked by mortar fire.

Cities, towns, villages, homesteads,
Pulverised, deserted,
Like forests chopped to the ground,
Amid the dead carcasses of the unburied.

Refugees, bandaged, huddled,lie unsheltered.
Everything is blasted into a shambles.
Lands smoulder in twisted chaos,
Regions plunged into darkness and cruelty.

Had it been tidal seas, brimming floods,
Earthquakes, volcanoes, hurricanes,
Some natural disaster;
You, who moulded our planet,
Would understand
Stretch out your hand
Through caring agencies and
Take pity on them.

But no Lord,
It was inter-racial strife,
Ethnic cleansing,
Unfettered nationalism,
Proud nations who misuse your name,
The evil fruits of power and greed,
'They have made a desert and then call it peace.'

Arise, O Lord, and defend your cause.
As a united people, may we bear each other's burdens!

Reflection from Psalm NOS 75 & 76

People who com-plain about God delaying so long before acting and permitting so much evil in the world, do well to examine their own lives and actions.

JUDGE OF THE NATIONS

O Lord, how impatient we can become!
Depravity is so extensive;
Justice, seems long delayed,
The suffering of the innocent,unceasing.

We grow sorely tempted to murmur;
'Why is the all-powerful ruler of our world
indifferent to the affairs of earth?
Is he not moved by the groans of his children?'

Yet, we know in our hearts that,
You, Lord, are the great provider,
Your plans are beyond our scrutiny,
You are wisdom itself.

What seems disordered now,
Is due to our own folly,
We are but instruments in your hands,
Almoners of your bounty.

Look into our actions, Lord,
How slow and tolerant we are
To amend within.
How impatient to reform without!

  'Your name is brought very near to us
  in the story of your wonderful deeds.' PS 75:1

Glory be ...

Reflection From Psalm NO 77

The Psalmist here complains to God for apparently having abandoned his people. But reflecting on Israel's past history, he finds consolation and feels that all will yet be well.

THE RIGHT HAND OF THE MOST HIGH

I cry out to the Lord,
Oh! that He would listen to my voice.
My unease is that the
Right hand of the Most High has been withheld.

Can it be that God will never again
Show us his old kindness?
There can be no joy for me now,
No sleep, until he acts.

All night long I pray.
My heart feels empty.
My soul as dry as dust;
Steeled as I am against all consolation.

I keep thinking of the good old days,
The mighty deeds of the Lord, and
How all nature reflected his glory.
How swift was his answer to entreaty!
He led his people along the way like sheep.
He gave them Moses and Aron as shepherds.
Past favours of the Lord reassure me,
That soon, he will answer my prayer.

  'You are the God that does marvellous deeds, .
  … with your own arm redeeming your people.' PS 77:14, 15

Glory be …

Reflection From Psalm NO 78

The journey of God's Chosen People from Egypt to Canaan is a symbol of our own lives from birth to death, from sin to redemption, from captivity to liberation.

REMEMBERING

Remember God's dealing with his people!
Hand it on from generation to generation.
We can forget so easily the lessons of the past,
Fall so quickly into the same pitfalls.

Israel's core offences were selfishness and pride.
Her eyes were cast inward.
She thought only of receiving,
Gloried only in possessions.

Favours were received with scant gratitude.
Soon they were forgotten.
Calamities incurred through transgression,
Taught only partial and passing lessons.

Like a gracious father,
The Lord looked lovingly on them;
He recognised there his own children,
Fashioned in his own image.
How dear they were to him,
Despite their folly!

The Lord considered their frail natures,
Their trials and sufferings,
The brevity of their passing lives.
He yielded to their appeal for mercy.
He restrained his uplifted hand.

So persistent was their waywardness,
So stubborn their ways of acting;
That the Ark, their glory,
Fell into enemy hands.

Suddenly, as from a deep sleep,
God rose up against their oppressors.
He no longer tolerated their sufferings.
The persecuting Philistines were routed,
The Ark restored, its abode on Sion.

'He chose David to shepherd his people.
His was the loyal heart that should tend them.
His was the skillful hand that should be their guide.' PS 78:72

Glory be …

Reflection from Psalm NO 79

Life deals an uneven hand to earth's children. Fortunately God shows no partiality to race, colour or creed. All who respond are precious to him.

LIFE IS NOT FAIR, BUT GOD IS

Lord, in the calamities,
Tragedies and disasters of life,
My thoughts turn to you.
Do not now hold us guilty
For our former sins.

I feel deeply for all who suffer,
Especially for those of little faith.
Are not all peoples of earth your children?
Do you not allot to each,
In the thousand accidents of place and birth,
An individual providence?

Are not your attributes of
Love, kindness, pity and mercy,
The same for all of us?
Why then should some be allowed to say;
'Where is our God?'

The light of faith shines brightest,
Against the darkest background.
God shows no partiality.
All who place their lives in his hands,
All who respond to his word,
Are precious to him.

'We, your people are the sheep of your pasture,
We will thank you forever and ever.' PS 79:13

Glory be …

Reflection from Psalm NO 80

The Church has often been compared to a vine. The allegory of the vine and the branches, aptly portrays the relationship between Christ and his members.

THE VINE
(A Prayer for the Church)

O God, restore us to our own.
Smile on us and we shall be saved.
You it was who tilled the soil,
That your Church, your vine, should flourish.
It struck root and encircled the globe.

Through inspired leadership,
You led her.
Marvellous the happenings that
Followed in her trail.
Her offspring you fed with
The finest nourishment.
The poor found shelter in her shade.

But today, some are unsettled in her ranks.
They feel uncared for and confused.
Others walk no more with us. They say;
'They no longer meet our needs.'

O God, restore the wall around your vineyard.
Renew your Church and revive your servants.
Nurture and guard what your own hand has planted.
Safeguard those you have chosen.
Affirm those you have made strong.

Never again will we turn away from you.
With a spirit renewed,
In your inspired word of yesterday,
We shall call on your holy name,
For the vital needs of our day.

   'Visit this vine; protect what your own hand has planted.' PS 80:15

Glory be ...

Reflection from Psalm NO 81

A people who forget their origins lose their identity. That is why God's greatest commandment to Israel was to 'Remember Egypt'.

LEST WE FORGET!

Lord, may we never forget our roots!
That 'Rock from which we were hewn,' IS 51:1
Lest, overlooking our origins,
We lose our identity.

Remember Egypt!
When you brought us out of slavery.
And gained the further shore.

You broke our chains,
You tamed our vices,
You healed our wounds.
We to be your people,
You to be our God.

Full ears of wheat to nourish us;
Honey dripping from the rock,
Our hearts' content.

How often we take for granted
Our independence and our freedom,
Our human progress, social welfare,
Our common bond,
With each other and with you?

You gave us new life, Lord,
A new identity,
You made us,
Members of your chosen people.

We accept your mandate to remember.
Building hope for the future,
On the foundations of the past.

  'I am the Lord your God
    Who brought you from the land of Egypt.' PS 81:10

Reflection from Psalm NO 82

FAIR PLAY

God stands up to open heaven's court.
He pronounces judgement on the judges.
'Justice, justice, shall you pursue,'
Is the constant plea of the prophets:
'Do justice for the weak and the orphan,
Defend the afflicted and needy.' IS 42:3

Those who have been commissioned
To bring peace,
Have betrayed your trust.
The foundations of society
Have been shaken to the core.
The Lord is saying:
'Why are my people going hungry,
While you abound in my gifts?
I can touch them,
Only through you.'

Lord, give confidence to your people,
Kindle a ray of hope,
In a world,
That has lost its sense of fairness.

   'Let your justice roll on like a river,
   Honesty like an ever-flowing stream.' AMOS 5:24

Glory be ...

Reflection from Psalm NO 83

Sometimes we may feel that God has abandoned his care of the universe — so much evil abounds. This Psalm explores the phenomenon.

A TIME FOR ACTION

You are an active God, Lord!
From the instant of creation,
To your walking with your people,
You were a cloud by day,
A column of fire by night.

You opened up seas.
You brought down walls.
You won battles.
You ruled kingdoms.

Yours was the greatest power on earth.
People knew it and acknowledged it with awe.

Now, Lord, people do as they please.
Nations go their separate ways.
You are no longer their guiding star.

Have you given up on us, Lord,
That the world ignores you?
Why so silent, holding your peace?

At one time in my life,
You were as real to me as a close friend.
You took part in my plans.
You shared my joys and sorrows.

Now, for some time,
You have been silent.
I just keep doing the same things,
Out of routine, without conviction.
When I speak of you I speak of the past,
I talk from memory.

Break your silence, Lord.
Let the world know you are here,
That you are in charge.

> 'Let them know that you alone are God,
> Whose name is most high
> Over all the earth.' PS 83:18

Glory be …

Reflection from Psalm NO 84

People like to experience tangible evidence of the Lord's presence. It makes them feel at home at prayer in their favourite church. 'The love of God comes to us through symbols.' – Prof Seamus Ryan

LOVE OF GOD'S HOUSE

The sparrow has found its home,
And the swallow a nest for her brood.
How restless our hearts without you,
O Lord our God!
You alone give meaning to our lives.

I love the beauty of your house,
The place where your glory dwells.
I enjoy the experience of being physically near you,
To experience the symbols of the Living God.

Within your sanctuary,
You enrich us.
We draw strength as a pilgrim people;
Find springs of healing,
For an empty world.

You alone are all beauty.
You are the fountain of life.
The silence, music, incense,
Express the human spirit within,
Raising our hearts to
The Eternal Sanctuary.

'One day in your courts
is better than a thousand elsewhere.' PS 84:10

Glory be …

Reflection from Psalm NO 85

A VOICE THAT SPEAKS OF PEACE

Lord, you have poured out great blessings
On this land.
Peace your blessing on the human heart,
And the race of earth.
You, Lord, are the Prince of Peace:
Emmanuel, God with us.
You speak peace to your people;
A peace that unites,
Reconciles,
Gives joy.
The peace that was freely welcomed by a woman,
In the name of all humanity,
Peace, announced by angels,
Finds here on earth,
No lasting home.

We speak peace in our greetings, saying;
'Peace, peace, when there is no peace.' JER 6:14

'Let justice roll down like the waters.' AMOS 5:24
Then, that faithfulness that springs
From our lives;
Will blend with the kindness of our God.
Justice and peace will embrace,
The bridal of earth and sky.

   'Justice shall march before the Lord
   And peace will follow his steps.' PS 85:13

Glory be …

Reflection from Psalm NO 86

We ask for guidance in the important choices of our lives and in the passing options that make up the routine of the day, marking the direction in which our lives move.

MY GUIDING LIGHT

Bend down and hear my prayer, O Lord.
You are full of mercy
For all who ask your help.

I will call on you whenever troubles strike,
And you will come to my rescue.
All the nations you have made,
Will worship before you.
They will bring glory
To your holy name.

Today, Lord, I ask for guidance.
Teach me your way.
Help me to recognise my goals,
So I may walk in your truth
Your faithful care
My escort.

Break into my confusion.
Temper my moods and
Tame my instincts,
That I choose what is wise.

Whisper where you want me to go, Lord,
And I will go there.

'Show me, Lord, your way
So that I may walk in your truth.' PS 86:11

Glory be …

Reflection from Psalm NO 87

Children of every race come together because all have become one in the Lord. All are children of the same mother.

MOTHER OF ALL PEOPLES

This world is yours, Lord.

We are all one
In the mould of your fashioning.

You gather together
The children of every race,
All bonded in birth
As brothers and sisters.

Grant me a truly ecumenical spirit,
To love every person,
Respect all peoples,
Your presence living
In the hearts of all.

Strengthen my roots,
Deepen my sources,
Knit closer my alliance
To all humankind.

Place a mark, Lord,
In your register of peoples,
  'All find a home in me.' PS 87:7

Glory be ...

Reflection from Psalm NO 88

This is acknowledged to be the saddest of the Psalms – transposed in this interpretation as a prayer of one dying from the modern scourge of AIDS.

ONE SUFFERING FROM AIDS

O Lord, God my salvation!
Oh! listen to my cry for help.
The burden of loneliness
Lies heavy upon me.
Friend and neighbour you have taken away:
My one familiar is darkness.

Afflicted and close to death since youth,
I have suffered terrors and helplessness.
I am ready to depart this life.
They say I am a hopeless case.
They have left me here to die.

O Lord, I lift up my hands for mercy,
The sacred name of my God
On my lips.
My end frightens me with the black unknown.
Shorten now my trial
And restore me to life.

Friends and neighbours have gone,
The Lord,
My only companion.

Glory be …

Reflection from Psalm NO 89

One of the great truths that shines through the pages of the Bible is the wonderful fact that God first loved us. This Psalm contrasts God's steadfast love with our own fickle response.

GIFT AND PROMISE

I will sing forever, O Lord, of your love.

I will announce your faithfulness from age to age.
Who in the skies can compare with the Lord;
Who of the heaven-born is like him?
Yours are the heavens and the earth;
You founded the world and everything within.

When all is well with us,
We are prone to neglect your blessings;
Yours are the blessings of heaven,
The earth is full of your riches.

Your promises endure forever.
We walk in the light of your face.
Strength and faithfulness surround you;
Even when we neglect your counsel
And go our selfish ways.

Your love for us is steadfast.
You never forsake us.

  'I will keep my covenant and
  Be true to my promises.' PS 89:28

Glory be ...

Reflection from Psalm NO 90

The Psalmist contrasts the fleeting nature of our human lives with God's timelessness. His prayer is that God in his wisdom would enhance the lives of his beloved children.

NUMBERING OUR DAYS

Lord, bring home to us how brief life is.
Teach us to appreciate the value of time.

As the fading image of a waking dream, or as
A flower that blossomed in the morning,
But, by evening, had wilted;
Such, the fleeting character
Of all human existence.

Seventy or eighty, are
Our allotted length of years,
Yet most of them are sorrow and trouble;
Speeding by, they sweep us along.

With you Lord, there is no beginning or end.
One day is as a thousand years,
And a thousand years as one day.

Gentle your way, Lord,
Into our short span of life.
There lend meaning and value
To those days that remain.

Teach us to number our days.
May our future be as happy
As our past was sad.

'Teach us to count the days that are ours,
And we shall come to the heart of wisdom.' PS 90:12

Glory be …

Reflection from Psalm NO 91

Increasingly, people look for protection and security in their homes, on the street, even in their cars. We can often overlook the role of our Guardian Angels to protect us from dangers.

DANGER

We live under the shade of the Almighty.
We are sheltered by the God
Who is above all gods.
All our days are under his care.
His providence, like eagle's wings,
Shields us.

He orders his angels to protect us.
On life's singled trail,
They signpost the way.
We need not be afraid of the dark, or
Fear dangers in broad daylight.

As we wake each morning,
We hear his reassuring words:

  'Because you cling to me in love,
  Know me as I really am, and
  Talk to me as friend to friend.
  I will deliver you,
  Protect you, because
  You acknowledge my name.' PS 91:14

Glory be ...

Reflection from Psalm NO 92   *A song of optimism.*

STILL FULL OF SAP

It is good to give thanks to the Lord.
It is great to sing praises to him.
To announce his love in the morning,
And recall his truths at the fall of night.

It is a privilege to be in your service and
To form part of your people.
My heart thrills at the sight
Of all you have made.
I feel refreshed, restored
Because of your blessings.

The senseless ones are ruled by possessions,
Their cravings are never satisfied.
God's friends,
Tired and harassed for a while,
Are destined to flourish.

Like a tree,
Planted in God's own garden,
Tended by his personal care;
Even in old age,
They still bear fruit,
Still full of sap,
Still green.

  'Planted in the house of the Lord,
  they will flourish in the courts of our God,
  Still bearing fruit when they are old,
  Still full of sap, still green.' PS 92:14

Glory be ...

Reflection from Psalm NO 93

In a tumultous world like ours, the restless sea is a fair symbol.
'The voice of the sea speaks to the soul.'
– KATE CHOPIN

THE SEA

I like to look at the surging sea.
It reminds me of your majesty, Lord.
The mighty oceans thunder to praise you,
The primeval abyss
Where all life was formed.

You, Lord, are my king, my rock.
You are clothed in greatness and strength.
Like an island, the Lord on high is indomitable;
Pounded by earth's storms,
The heaving tide,
The foam,
The spray,
I sigh for your fixed abode.

You will soothe our fretful natures
And comfort our troubled spirits.

  'You will trample our sins underfoot
  And send them to the bottom of the sea.' MICAH 7:18-19

  'More majestic than the breakers of the sea,
  The Lord is majestic in the heights.' PS 93:4

Glory be …

Reflection from Psalm NO 94

We ask the Lord to teach us through the events of each day; how to decipher his messages in a chance encounter, in a piece of news, in a sudden joy, in a threatening worry.

EVIL

Lord, there are men and women
In this world of ours,
They hold no belief in God.
The very thought of a hereafter
Is anathema to them.

They delight in oppression and cruelty,
Torture, bloodshed and crime,
Their daily agenda;
The innocent, meek and poor,
Their hapless victims.

How long, O Lord, how long?
Do you take no notice?
How can we preserve our faith
In your government of the universe?

Our present life is a school.
Happy are those you teach,
Whom you train
By means of your commandments.

When my heart is troubled by villainy
Give me hope and confidence.
The perpetrators of evil,
Will be mired in their own misdeeds,
Their plans will come to nought.

  'The Lord will not abandon his people
  Nor will he forsake his heritage.' PS 94:23

Glory be …

Reflection from Psalm NO 95

Most probably this poem was intended to be recited at the beginning of the Sabbath worship, in order to awaken the fervour of the people who were attending the sacred functions in the Temple.

THE PLACE OF REST

Come before the Lord with thankful hearts.
Give a happy shout in honour
Of the Rock of our salvation.

Come, kneel before the Lord our maker.
We are his sheep, and
He is our shepherd.
Oh! that you would hear him calling you.

Don't harden your hearts,
As Israel did in the desert;
With their molten calf and
Incessant complaining.

For forty years the Lord watched them in disgust.
He swore, that they would never enter
The Promised Land. His frightful words:
'They shall not enter my rest.'

How many years for me Lord?
Make me see the ways
To attain my rest.

   'Oh! that we would hear him calling us.' PS 95:7

Glory be …

Reflection from Psalm NO 96

The Psalmist had a prophetic vision of the Messianic era. It was the acceptance of Christ as Messiah that furnished the reasons for rejoicing and the praise of God called for in this Psalm.

A NEW SONG

Sing a new song to the Lord.
Tell about his mighty deeds.
In the Lord's honour,
Let the whole earth be in unison.

Teach me to lilt a fresh tune.
To live a new life each morning;
Every minute, every hour,
A new hope to greet the dawn of each new day.

The earth has seen God's salvation to his people.
That is why the world breaks out in praise to their God;
That is why it sings for joy.

Tell the nations that the Lord reigns!
That the King of the universe is in charge!
Let the sea and the land, all nature,
Show His glory.
Let all creation be in harmony.

'Music has charms to soothe a savage breast.' WILLIAM CONGREVE

Glory be …

Reflection from Psalm NO 97

It is not easy to obtain genuine and deep joy in a world laden with sorrow. We need the eyes of faith.

REJOICE

Let me rejoice always in the Lord,
To show in my face the happiness
That comes from serving him.

Let all the earth rejoice!
That the Lord is their God
And they are his people.
His goodness and justice are
The foundations of his creation.

To be joyful where there is so much sorrow,
Is not easy, Lord.
Deepen my faith,
Gift me with a sense of humour.
Grant me patience, to see ...

That you, Lord, are present,
In the tenderness of your love,
In the fullness of your sovereignty,
In the pity of your compassion,
Through all trials and sufferings.

Thank you, Lord,
That I have brought a smile to others.
That I was the dawn of gladness
For honest hearts.

'May all who are godly be happy in the Lord.' PS 97:11

Glory be ...

Reflection from Psalm NO 98

HOPE

Lord, what prospect for peace today!
Must there be ever toil and tears,
Pain and sorrow,
Wars and bloodshed?

Shed a ray of hope, Lord,
A shaft of light that pierces the gloom.
That is the paradox of my life:
To have tension at times
But certitude always.

Look! What marvellous things you accomplished
For your people.
You made your salvation known
To the ends of the earth.

Past blessings bode future promise.
I belong to a victorious army
That in the end, will
Defeat all opposition and
Conquer the whole world.

Toil and sorrow will not last,
Nor can wars continue forever.

'Hope springs eternal in the human breast.' ALEXANDER POPE
The Lord, the font of all hopefulness.

Glory be ...

Reflection from Psalm NO 99

It is precisely because he is all holy that God is willing and eager to hear the prayers of his humble offspring and pardon their sins.

THE LORD IS HOLY

The Lord is King!
All nations stand in awe at his presence!
He sits between the guardian angels.
Let the whole earth tremble
Before the majesty of your pervasiveness.

Let all peoples hallow your holy name,
Because integrity is found in all you do.
Let all humanity bow before you in worship.

You, Lord, my king, are holy,
With a holiness beyond all my experience.
I have only images of your essence
Within the limits of my mind;
The purity of a mountain stream,
The path of the clouds,
The star-studded sky,
The falling of the pristine snow.

I ask for the sense of your holiness
To pervade my being.
I ask to be touched
With a spark of your fire.

'Holy, holy, holy Lord, God of power and might,
Heaven and earth are full of your glory.
Hosanna in the highest.' LITURGY

Glory be …

Reflection from Psalm NO 100

God cares for us as a shepherd his flock. He does give individual attention to each sheep and pays special attention to the one that most needs his care or who strays.

SHEEP OF GOD'S PASTURE

Go through his open gates with thanksgiving.
Come before God with joyful songs!
His faithfulness reaches all generations.

Make me feel a member of the flock, Lord,
Never let me think I can go it alone,
That the lives of others do not concern me.

Make me feel at home in your fold.
Lend me an attentive ear,
Not afraid to raise my voice
In song and in word.

I am a member of the flock,
Because you are the Shepherd.
Loyalty is the brand of your marking.
We belong to the Lord our Maker.

   'We are God's people,
   The sheep of his pasture.' PS 100:3

Glory be …

Reflection from Psalm NO 101

Grateful to God and conscious of the heavy responsibility that now rested upon him, David was zealous to rid the city and his court of the abuses and corruption that had darkened the closing years of Saul's reign. This Psalm is now adapted in the form of New Year Resolutions.

COMMITMENT

Lord, How I would like to reform everyone!
Free the city of God from all evil.
But, you know me so well,
My life is an open book.

First, let me begin at home,
With myself;
These thoughts, my firm resolve.

'I will try to walk a blameless path.
But how I need your help!
I need it most in my own home,
For there I wish to act as I should.
Help me to refuse the low and bad things;
To hate all crooked deals of every kind.
I will reject selfishness and
Stay far from every evil.
Whoever secretly slanders a neighbour
I will reduce to silence.'

They are a bit vague, Lord,
Not very specific;
Oh! yes, Let me not forget you:

  'I will sing of mercy and justice;
  To you, Lord, I will sing praise!
  I will walk in the path of integrity;
  Oh when will you come to me?' PS 101:1-2

Glory be ...

Reflection from Psalm NO 102

JERUSALEM
(Where the Messiah was to die and be raised)

So many travelled to the temple in Jerusalem
They went there to give glory to the Lord.
His praises were sung throughout the city.
Many pilgrims from near and far
Came to worship him.

I know you will come
And have mercy on Jerusalem.
Now is the time to pity her,
Now the era for your pledged assistance.

Your people love every stone in her walls.
They cherish every grain of dust in her streets,
Their houses anointed by the presence of humankind.
The time has come to have mercy on Jerusalem.

For the Lord will rebuild the Holy City.
He will come in his glory!
Let this be recorded for the generations to come,
That a people yet unborn may praise the Lord.
Tell them that God looked down from his Temple in heaven.
He heard the cries of his people in slavery.
They were children of death, and he let them go.

  'But you never grow old.
  You are forever, and your years never end.' PS 102:27

Glory be ...

Reflection from Psalm NO 103

A hymn of praise and thanksgiving to God for his many benefits and blessings bestowed on all frail mortals who try their best.

COMPASSION

Remember all the Lord has accomplished for you.
He pardons all your sins and
Over body and soul
He extends his healing hands.

Your very bones will rejoice
As you feel the blessing of his mercy,
In the depth of your being.

He is merciful and tender towards
Those who don't deserve it.
He is slow to get angry and
Rich in faithful love.
The Lord acts with integrity.
He is compassionate towards
All who are oppressed.

You will feel your youth renewed,
As the eagle's plumage is restored.
As far as the east is from the west,
So far does he remove our offenses from us.

   'He is like a father to us.
   He is tender and kind to those who honour him.' PS 103:13

Glory be …

Reflection from Psalm NO 104

When we look at creation we hear the one discordant note that fails to harmonise with the work of the Creator – the sinfulness of humankind.

HARMONY

O God, how beautiful is the world
You created for our habitation!
Even before we were fashioned from the dust,
You prepared a place in which we live and grow.
You open up your hand and provide all we need.
You stretched out the starry curtain of the heavens.
You cut out the surface of the earth
To make the seas.

You send rain upon the mountains.
The valleys are decked with grain.
You gave the moon for our calendar.
You told the sun to mark the days.

Everything created is in harmony, Lord,
Balance and consistency
The hallmark of your crafting.

> 'You send out your Spirit, they are created;
> And you renew the face of the earth.' PS 104:30

Glory be …

Reflection from Psalm NO 105

Here the Psalmist wishes to recall God's gratuitous goodness to us and through us to others. A theme later enlarged and developed in the New Testament.

'NEVER HURT THEM'

Lord, the history of your chosen ones
Is the story of your care for me.
Today I am anxious about the future,
My own and those I love.

I look to you and your strength.
I search for your face in
My brothers and sisters,
The promise of protection:
'Lay no hand on them,
Never hurt them, my chosen ones.'

You take what is done to you,
What is done to me.
You make me one with you.

Your word protecting me.
Your warning defending me.
Your promise guiding me.

You have looked after me, Lord,
Through difficult times.
You will secure and shepherd me,
Through the perilous future.

   'Do not touch those I have anointed,
   do no harm to any of my prophets.' PS 105:15

Glory be ...

Reflection From Psalm No 106

*In our impatience
we could fail to give
due thanks for past
blessings.*

OUR SHORT MEMORIES

Thank you, Lord, how good you are!
Your love endures forever.
Who can ever list your great deeds,
Praise you even half enough?

Our ancestors soon forgot,
Your many acts of kindness.
Even so, you saved them,
To defend the honour of your name.

I, too, have a short memory, Lord.
I have accepted your gifts,
Without reference to the Giver.
Whenever a crisis was over,
I went back to my old selfish ways.

I forgot that every act of yours,
Is not only an action
But a message,
A promise of deliverance forever.
Now, teach me to read into my actions
The message of your love.

How patient is my God,
Even when I fail him!

'Remember always his steadfast love'
My daily mantra. PS 106:4

Reflection from Psalm NO 107

The ancient people list four dangers: desert, prison, sickness and storm at sea. These are reflected in this Psalm.

DANGERS AND DELIVERANCES

From the deserts of life to the fortified city
Lord, I have wandered in the parched deserts,
Missing the way to the city that was my home.
Hungry and thirsty, so that my spirit died within me:
Guide me in the right path to that city where you dwell.

From life's prisons to light and freedom
I have lain down where darkness overshadowed me,
Helpless in bonds, my heart bent down in sorrow.
With no one to aid me in my weakness,
I cried out to the Lord and He rescued me.

From sickness to health
I lay sick, with no stomach for food,
I was close to death's door.
I cried out to the Lord in my weakness,
He uttered the word of healing, and
He saved me from peril.

From life's storms to the safety of a harbour
The storm wind rises, churning up its waves,
So, I cried out to the Lord,
He relieved my distress;
Stilling the storm into a whisper.
He brought me to the haven
Where I longed to be.

Glory be …

Reflection from Psalm NO 108

REPETITION
(This Psalm-prayer is put together from Psalms 57:1-11, 60:5-12)

So often I repeat myself in my prayer,
As you yourself, Lord, repeat yourself in your word.
I realise that life itself is a repetition
A retelling, a rerun, a reiteration.

My refrain of praise
Echoes like a bird-song
Through the valleys of my being.

My life, Lord, is made up of patches,
Of old experiences lived out anew,
Within the framework of my existence.

It is love that makes repetition pleasurable.
Grant me that faithful love,
To see each new morning,
Every familiar experience,
The bread I receive from your hands,
As a fresh event.

'Don't mind my repetitions, Lord,
As I don't mind yours.' CARLOS G. VALLES

Glory be …

Reflection from Psalm NO 109

THE WEAPON OF THE POOR

Lord, we do not understand curses
Because we do not understand the poor.
Who know in their bones that they
Are the victims of injustice.

They are powerless, without money,
Without influence; unlike others,
Who muscle their way to the top,
To get what they want.

They have no weapons,
Only the rapier of the word;
Each barb, a curse, a warning,
What God would do
When there is no redress.

May these words,
Hit their target,
Stem injustice,
Bring peace to the poor you love, Lord.

'For he stands at the right hand of the needy ones
To save their lives from those who condemn them.' PS 109:31

Glory be …

Reflection from Psalm NO 110

A PRAYER FOR PRIESTS

Remember your anointed, Lord,
Who sit at your right hand.
They are priests forever after the
Order of Melchizedek.

The mysterious appearance of this king,
Who bears bread and wine
And blesses Abraham
In whom all faithful are also blessed;
Bringing heaven down
To the altars of earth.

May they never prove unworthy
Of your trust.
May your sacred words
Accompany them with love,
Every day of their lives.

'You are a priest forever according to the order of Melchizedek.'
PS 110:4

Glory be ...

Reflection from Psalm NO III

PRAYING TOGETHER

I do not pray alone, Lord,
I pray with my brothers and sisters,
Who work together
For the coming of your kingdom.

I make mine the prayers of each,
While they make my prayers their own,
Giving prayer a new meaning,
A new dimension,
A new depth.

Even getting together in your presence, Lord,
Is itself a prayer. When we pray,
The whole world prays.
We know its needs,
We live its aspirations.

All who suffer the same evils
Need the same blessings.
There is no selfishness in common prayer.

Bless our group, Lord.
As we struggle for unity.
Bless the efforts we make
To bring us together.

'I give thanks to you, Lord, with all my heart in the meeting of
The just and their assembly' PS III:1

Glory be ...

Reflection from Psalm no 112

*'The simplicity of a
true heart will find
the shortcuts to
holiness.'*

A Portrait of the Just

Lord, we are all made in your image.
The just more closely resembles their Maker,
Faithful love, the root and foundation
Of their thoughts and actions.

Light rises in the darkness for the just,
Who is gracious, merciful and honest.
All goes well for those who lend generously
And conduct their affairs with integrity.

Their hearts are steady, they have no fear,
Lavishly they give to the poor.
They are not afraid of bad tidings;
For all time to come they will be remembered.

Sometimes, we make life too complicated, Lord.
We don't need the latest book to find you.
Grant us humility of mind
And simplicity of spirit.
Oh! to have it said by friends and neighbours,
As they depart from my grave:
'He/she was a just man/ woman.'

'For all time to come the just will not stumble.' ps 112:6

Glory be …

Reflection From Psalm NO 113

Like the future St Paul, the Psalmist discovered that Good manifests himself more readily through the weak and lowly.

STRENGTH IN WEAKNESS

Lord, your strength is made known in weakness.
When we lift our heads high in pride,
We will be humbled.
You fill the empty vessel
With the fullness of your power.

The wisdom of the wise is confounded.
The cleverness of the clever is destroyed.
The glory of God shines in our lowliness.

Let me feel the joy of your Spirit
When I speak in your name,
When I act in your cause.
I have to disappear that you may appear.
I must diminish that you may increase.

  'His throne is set on high,
  But he stoops to look down on heaven and earth.' PS 113:6

Glory be …

Reflection from Psalm NOS 114 & 115

We tend to be moulded towards the objects of our worship. If we bow before riches, we assume the characteristics of their nature and grow in hardness of heart, insensitive to the needs of our brothers and sisters around us.

IDOLS

Lord, the dark night of exile and suffering
For your chosen people,
Which appeared to have no end
Suddenly came to a close, and
Israel was free.

You were with your people in the past,
You are nearer your loved ones today.

You warned us, Lord, of the error
Of placing idols on our altars:
The idols of silver and gold,
The work of human hands.
Your admonition:
'Their makers will end up like them,
so are all who trust in them.' PS 115:8

What idols do I worship, Lord,
That I become insensitive to you
And the needs of my brothers and sisters?

Will I become like them
A dumb idol in society?

Oh! to bless and live
As your faithful servant.
To grow and increase
In the likeness of you!

Free me from all idols in my life,
That I may walk freely again.

Glory be ...

Reflection from Psalm NO 116

A prayer of thanks-giving of one pre-served from death.

PASSION & RESURRECTION
(The Psalm was prayed on the way to Gethsemane)

I love the Lord because he hears my prayers.
He bends down and listens.
So I will pray as long as I breathe!

Death stared me in the face.
I was afraid and sad.
Then I cried, 'Lord, save me!'
How kind he is!
How good he is!
This God of ours is so merciful!

I was facing death and then he saved me.
Now I can rest.
For the Lord has done this miracle for me.
He has saved me from death.
He has dried my eyes from tears,
My feet from stumbling,
That I may walk before you, Lord,
In the land of the living.

What return can I make,
For all the good Lord has done for me?
I will lift up the cup of salvation
And call on the name of the Lord.

I will bring him the sacrifice I promised.
I will do this in front of all the people.
His loved ones are very special to him.
He does not lightly let them die.

O Lord, you have freed me from my chains.
I will serve you forever.

I will worship you always.
I will give you a sacrifice of thanks ...

'They surrounded me with the snares of death.
With the anguish of the tomb they caught me.
In sorrow and distress I called on the Lord's name.' PS 116:3-4

Glory be ...

Reflection from Psalm NO 117

We have an invitation to link-up with all nations to praise God for his goodness. The blessings accorded to the Chosen People were intended ultimately for everyone.

SALVATION FOR ALL

Lord, may I never fall into the trap,
Of excluding even one human being
From the blessings of salvation,
Intended for the whole of humanity.

There is but one family
To which all humankind belongs.

May the way I live my life
Be a welcoming invitation
And never an obstacle for others,
To acclaim the Lord forever.

'For the Lord's faithful love is mighty,
His truth goes on forever.
Praise the Lord!' PS 117:2

Glory be ...

Reflection from Psalm NO 118

A DAY OF THE LORD

Lord, teach me not to fear humankind.
Since you are my helper,
No mortal can inflict
Lasting evil on me.

Even were help refused or yet delayed;
It is for my greater good,
Providing an opportunity:
To repent of sin,
To increase my prayer,
To grow in the likeness
Of my Lord and master.

May every day be the day of the Lord in my life!

A day of victory and praise,
A day of rejoicing and thanksgiving,
A day of conquest of sin,
A day to prepare for eternity.

   'This is the day the Lord has made.
   Let us rejoice and be glad in it.' PS 118:24

Glory be …

Every day is a day made memorable by God. A day in which the Lord has acted. If I am alive it is because God is acting in me with his infinite power and merciful grace.

Reflection from Psalm NO 119A

The Psalmist is enamoured with the surpassing excellence of the Divine Law, and is thrilled at the thought of the deep sense of peace and blessedness that is theirs who observe its precepts.

GOD'S WAY TO OUR PEACE

Happy are all who follow the laws of God.
Happy are all who search for God.
They always choose to do his will.
They can do no evil.

The will of the Lord is the secret of our peace.
Allured and deceived by other attractions,
We forfeit the blessedness of serenity.
We wander in paths that lead to pain and grief.

Perfect observance of God's laws
Is beyond our unaided nature, so
I have stored them in my heart.
I have pondered well on them in my mind.

God's law is our protection and shield,
Our strength against attack.
Wrong ways lead away from our true goal,
Distract us from the real source of help.

Oh! how I need divine light and guidance,
To follow what truly pleases the Lord.

 'Blessed are those who keep your instructions,
 Who seek you with their whole heart.' PS 119:12

Glory be …

Reflection from Psalm NO 119B

GOD'S WAY – OUR LIGHT

Walking your ways, Lord,
Is not as one pleases, but
What I ought to do.
Your path is more precious
Than gold and silver.

Your word is a lamp to my feet,
A light to illuminate the way before me.
Lord, gift me with common sense.
Help me to apply your rules
To all I do and say.

In distress and confusion
Your commands are a comfort to me.
Your laws are always fair.
All your commands are based on truth.

To see you in all things,
To discipher your will in all events
Is my way to wisdom
Happiness and peace.

'Your words are a lamp to light the path ahead of me.' PS 119:105

Glory be ...

Reflection from Psalm NO 120

Human beings having to flee from other human beings – whole groups of people uprooted from their homes and lands; exiles, expatriates and refugees, is the sin of our civilisation.

AN EXILE'S PRAYER

I pray today, Lord, for myself and fellow exiles.
Those who love their homes
But are forced to live in strange surroundings,
With people we do not know;
Who speak a language we do not understand.

I pray for all those who have been deprived of:
Their right to live in their own territories;
Those who were forcibly ejected,
Discriminated against,
Persecuted,
Expelled.
Those who dream of a promised land,
But are now camping in shanty towns.

I pray that we may feel exiles no longer.
That we make ourselves at home
Wherever we are,
In the warmth of our hope
And the strength of our faith.

  'Only this, to do what is right,
  To love loyalty and to walk humbly with your God.' MICAH 6:8

Glory be …

Reflection from Psalm NO 121

A splendid picture of the paternal goodness of God and his wonderful providence over his people as they journey towards Jerusalem.

A PILGRIM PEOPLE

Lord, your people journeyed yearly to
    Jerusalem.
Within the Temple they worshipped in prayer and sacrifice.
The Sanctuary was the holiest place on earth,
The symbol of your presence among them.

I too am on pilgrimage,
A member of your pilgrim people.
I journey through life towards
The eternal Jerusalem, the heaven
I hope for at the end of my days on earth.

You know my weaknesses,
The dangers on the road.
Stand at my right side.
Guard me from all evil.
Watch over me day and night.

May the Lord guard my life.
May he preserve me from accidents.
May he protect my journeying.
May he guide me to his home.

You, Lord, are my keeper,
In the strength of your assured word,
I will go bravely and cheerfully
On to the end.
I am confident that all will be well for me,
Now and forever.

  'The Lord will guard your goings and comings
   Henceforth unto eternity.' PS 121:8

Glory be …

Reflection from Psalm NO 122

PEACE IN JERUSALEM

O Lord, dear to the Psalmist
Beyond words to express it
Was the Holy City.
There were the Temple and sanctuary
Of the one true God.

I pray today for peace.
Peace for your Holy City
Jerusalem.

King David installed there, the
Ark of the Covenant,
Symbol of your presence
Among your people.

You intended it as a city,
Where people gathered together
In unity and concord.
But its stones have known
No lasting peace.

Armed soldiers patrol her streets,
It's a divided city,
A city of tension.

O Jerusalem, may there be peace
Within your walls.
This I ask for the sake of all
My brothers and sisters.
I ask it for all who live there.

> 'May they pray for your peace, Jerusalem...
> I will say, 'Peace be within you!' PS 122:6-7

Dear to the Psalmist, beyond words to express it, was Jerusalem, because there were the Sanctuary and the Temple of the one true God. Later it became the city where the Messiah suffered, died and rose for our salvation.

Reflection from Psalm NO 123

Our eyes are the most expressive sense of all our faculties. Lord Byron wrote; 'And oh! that eye was in itself a soul!'

OUR EYES

This morning,
I raise my eyes to you, Lord.
These precious orbs you gifted all:

To behold the wonders of creation,
To see your face;
In the chuckle of a child,
In the smile of a friend,
In the frown of a senior,
In the sightlessness of the blind.

My eyes can speak too!
A twinkle can express volumes,
A loving regard, affection.
A leer, suspicion, disdain.

Today,
My eyes are turned to you, Lord;
And that is a prayer.

   'So our eyes are on the Lord our God
   Till he show us his mercy.' PS 123:2

Glory be ...

Reflection from Psalm NO 124

How often life has turned out so much better, especially when we have escaped the consequences of our own imprudence!

THE TRAP

I look back on those events in my life, Lord,
When it seems I was caught in a trap. When
'The thing I greatly feared had come upon me.' JOB 3:25
I was in a catch-22, quandary,
With no clear solution to my problems.

Today as I reflect on those dark hours,
Now that I am at peace, with you,
With my calling in life,
With the people around me,
My heart is filled with gratitude.

It was you, Lord, who were beside me
All the time.
I could have been tempted to despair,
Eaten up by anger,
Destroyed by hatred,
Buried under pride.

Instead I have slipped away with my life!

'Like a bird that escapes
From the fowler's trap.
The trap was broken
And I was freed.!' PS 124:7

   'Our help comes from the Lord,
   The maker of heaven and earth.' PS 124:8

Glory be ...

Reflection from Psalm NO 125

Here the Psalmist contrasts the stead-fastness of a moun-tain with our own vacillating nature.

THE MOUNTAIN

People are fascinated by mountains, Lord.
They want to scale them to their summits,
Pit their skills, energies and endurance;
Against their craggy fissures.

Would that I could have the steadfastness
Of the mountains in my life, Lord;
That endurance that wins through!

I am so inconstant,
The winds of adversity shake me,
I waver, I hesitate, I doubt.
I begin with enthusiasm,
But fall down half way.

  'Those who trust in the Lord
  Are as steady as Mount Zion.
  They are not moved
  When troubles come.' PS 125:1

Glory be …

Reflection from Psalm NO 126

The greening and flourishing plant life where formerly there had been a dry barren waste, provides a symbol of hope for the Psalmist.

WADIS

You speak to us through the image of wadis, Lord,

Those baked-dry riverbeds
That spring to life in flash-floods,
Greening the surrounding terrain;
'May we be made fresh as streams in the desert.'

Come into my life, Lord.
Release the streams of grace.
Encourage me through new insights,
In the silence of my heart,
In the meditation of my mind:
To let in:
'New light through chinks that time has made.' WILLIAM BLAKE

That a tired, jaded, burnt-out life,
Might touch and refresh the lives of others,
With your ablution of love.

   'Restore our fortunes, O Lord,
   Like the streams of the Negeb!' PS 126:4

Glory be ...

Reflection from Psalm NO 127

*We can allow our
work to so completely
overwhelm us that
we lose perspective
in other areas of life.
It's a contemporary
respectable fault.*

THE WORKAHOLIC

Lord, I thank you for this timely reminder,
I work too much.
I believe myself to be indispensable.
Hard work for me is an addiction.
Except that it has a respectable name.

When earthly goods have at last
Been amassed, there is still no rest.
The same amount of labour
I spent to acquire them,
Must now be expended
If they are to be retained.

I am caught up in a treadmill
Of ceaseless activity.

Help me now to work
With you in mind.
The loving awareness of my
Dependence on you, your caution:
'If the Lord does not build the house,
In vain do its builders labour.' PS 127:1
You alone, Lord,
Can give peace and contentment.
Teach me to be quiet and resigned
That the fruits of my life,
Are what God wants them to be.

It is foolish to work hard
From morning till night.
For God wants his loved ones,
To have the proper rest.

[144]

'In vain you get up earlier,
Put off going to bed…
For it is the Reliable who provides
For the chosen ones as they sleep.' PS 127:2

Glory be …

Reflection from Psalm NO 128

Sharing a meal together can deepen family bonds and nurture friendships.

MEALS TOGETHER

Lord, how blessed it is
To have meals together!

If we learn to pray together
And eat together;
We will learn the art
Of living together.

No more fast foods for me, Lord!
Each meal has its ritual too.
Each morsel its due reverence.
It is God's reward for those
Who respect and trust him.

Has not heaven been compared to a banquet?
Then every meal is a rehearsal.

  'You will eat the fruit of your labour
  And may the Lord bless you
  All the days of your life.' PS 128:2

Glory be …

Reflection from Psalm NO 129

Anyone who imagines he/she is liked by all is living in a fool's paradise.

ENEMIES

I may not like to know it, Lord,
But I do have enemies.
Not everyone likes me.
I am not everyone's friend.

There are people who are
Unsympathetic towards me,
Dislike me, oppose me,
Hinder my work,
Who rejoice when I fail,
Feel sad when I succeed,
Speak ill of me.
Give me frosty looks.
Always take the adversary position.

I bear the marks of enmity
Within my soul.
Help me, Lord,
To accept the reality of my sufferings,
Without bitterness or retaliation.

The fact that I have enemies,
Humbles and chastens me.

Lord, help me to learn about myself,
From those who are ill-disposed towards me.
They reveal more about my weak points,
Than those who smother me with affection.

It's encouraging to know, Lord, that,

   'My enemies have never been able to finish me off!' PS 129:2

Glory be ...

Reflection from Psalm NO 130

Deeply conscious of sin and the wretchedness of soul that sin entails, the Psalmist feels he does not deserve pardon, yet he knows it will be granted.

OUT OF THE DEPTHS

Out of the depths I cry to you, O Lord.
I make my prayer to you, from the depths of my heart.
I am profoundly conscious of my own sinfulness.
I have reaped the woeful harvest
Of my own bad sowing.

There is no escape for me now, except,
Through the merciful help
Of my offended Lord.

I see and read daily about the
Appaling crimes, cruelties
And atrocities of humankind.
And I reflect:
'There go I, but for the grace of God.'

I sometimes think, Lord, that if
You made us incapable of evil
All would be peace and tranquillity.
But then, Lord, we would not
Have fitted into your
Master plan of creation.

Lord, do you keep in mind all our sins?
If you do, then who could survive?
But you are a forgiving God, and
What a consoling thought that is!

  'I long for his forgiveness
  More than the night watchman longs
  For the dawn of day.' PS 130:6-8

Glory be ...

Reflection from Psalm NO 131

With a proliferation of prayer methods and manuals on how to pray, we could overlook the dictum; 'Keep it simple.'

SIMPLICITY

I have used too many words in my prayers, Lord.
I have tried to fit in too many ideas.
I employ too many arguments.
I have tried to get my prayer,
All neatly tidied-up.
I have kept my eye on the clock.

Now I need to return
To the simplicity of childhood.
Not childish, but childlike.

Could it be that I have made the intellect
You gave me to find you,
An obstacle to seeing you?

I don't think myself better than others.
I don't pretend to know it all.
I am quiet now before the Lord,
The thoughts of a child on its mother's breast,
A child's thoughts were all my soul knew.

   'I have kept my whole being quiet and silent,
   Like an infant quieted at its mother's breast,
   Like an infant quieted in my whole being.' PS 131:2

Glory be ...

Reflection from Psalm NO 132

How can we sleep comfortably in our beds when our brothers and sisters lie in the open under a ruthless sky?

SYMBOL AND REALITY

Lord, your servant David could not bear,
That the Ark of the Lord
Should rest under a tent,
While he had a king's palace.

But he lived to see the Ark,
Rescued from its wanderings and
Placed in the Tabernacle
On Mount Zion.

It was not until the Ark,
The symbol of your presence
Had been placed in the
Holy of Holies that
Your glory filled the vast Temple.

Today, Lord, we have your Real Presence
In the Holy Eucharist
On altars around the world.
It is now your resting place on earth.
There you have chosen to live among us.

'Let us go to the place of his dwelling;
Let us go to kneel at his footstool.' PS 132:7

Glory be …

Reflection from Psalm NO 133

The harmonious dwelling together of people dedicated to the service of the Lord is the theme of this Psalm. As a result the whole nation is refreshed and quickened in its social and religious spirit.

DWELLING UNITED

What a graphic picture you draw,
Through the pen of your Psalmist, Lord,
Of the pleasant atmosphere that should prevail,
Where families dwell together?

It should be like a
Precious aromatic oil
That diffuses a
Sweet-smelling fragrance.

and

As a refreshing dew that
Falls overnight
On high mountains.

Yet, Lord, how often is this true?

I pray for every family,
I pray for my own,
I pray for all
Mothers and fathers,
Brothers and sisters
In the world; that,
Family love and unity
May occupy
A blessed home
In the hearts of all.

> 'How very good, how delightful it is
> When kindred live together in unity!
> It is like a precious oil on the head …
> It is like the dew of Hermon.' PS 133:1-2

Glory be …

Reflection from Psalm NO 134

A prayer for those who are obliged to work during the hours of darkness.

THE NIGHT

You cover us with darkness, Lord,
To afford us rest,
To renew our energies,
To prepare for a new day.
'Our little life is rounded with a sleep.' SHAKESPEARE

I pray for all those whose duties
Oblige them to turn
Night into day,
Who must work
While the rest of us sleep.

I pray for those who cannot find rest,
But toss and turn,
Those who worry a great deal,
Having active minds
In tired bodies.

I pray for those who
Keep vigil through the night hours;
Proclaiming you Lord of the day and the night,
With their presence.

'Lift up your hands to the Holy Place
And bless the Lord through the watches of the night.' PS 134:1, 2

Glory be ...

Reflection from Psalm NO 135

*Obstacles on the
road to progress
need not impede,
but rather challenge
the resourcefulness of
the Christian spirit.*

THE TYRANT KINGS

It is easy and pleasant to sing the praises
Of the one we love.
You have been good to me, Lord,
You have chosen me as your own possession.

But I know well my own weaknesses,
How prone I am to forsake you,
Follow after and worship other gods:
The pleasures of the flesh,
Fleeting earthly rewards,
Pandering to the flattery of others.

As once your people were opposed by tyrant kings,
On their pilgrim journey towards the Promised Land;
Og and Sihon, who obstructed them, barring their way.
So, my progress towards you, Lord,
Was blocked by:
Dangers I have experienced,
Disappointments I have met,
Moments when it seemed,
All chances were over.

Then, a mighty hand opened for me again,
Renewed my hopes,
Bestowed courage.

I have my own names too,
My own memories,
My history is written on the palm of your hand.

No more obstacles will now frighten me.
I will remember your conquest of Og and Sihon.
With you by my side, Lord,
My way will be open to the end!

'He it was that slew the kings in their pride,
Sehon king of the Amorrhites, and Og the king of Basan.' PS 135:10, 11

Glory be …

Reflection from Psalm NO 136

One of the most marvellous truths that slowly grows upon us is that God is a tremendous lover who pursues us throughout life; 'God first loved us' and we are touched by his loving designs.

HIS LOVING KINDNESS

Now I know, Lord, the eternal secret.
Why you spread out our planet above the waters,
How you brought your people through mighty wonders,
Out of Egypt and into the Promised Land.

It is your loving kindness.

Creation, and life support,
All visible things,
Are the result and witness
Of a loving kindness
That endures forever.

As your beloved disciple was later to express it;
'God is love.' I JN 4:8

May I too have my personal litany, Lord?

You brought me to life,
You placed me in a loving family,
You taught me to pronounce your name,
You opened your word to me in the Scriptures,
You called me to the service of your people,
You give joy to my heart,
You have called me your friend.

All this because of
Your loving kindness,
That will last forever.

   'O give thanks to the God of heaven,
   Whose faithful love endures forever.' PS 136:26

Glory be …

Reflection from Psalm NO 137

PARADOX

This is the enigma of life, Lord.

How can I sing while others weep?
How can I make merry while others mourn?
How can I eat well when others starve?
How can I rest while others toil?
How can I speak of happiness
When others are in misery?

Does not music require a suitable spirit
On the part of those who make it?

May I be sensitive, Lord,
To the pain of those around me?
The agony of millions
In the face of hunger, destitution, and death?
Those who are scarred by the violence of wars?

We are exiles here, Lord,
There is a time for joy, but also,
A time for responsibility,
To alleviate suffering.
A time to restore peace.

Bring joy, Lord, to the nations
That now cannot sing.

'How could we sing a song of the Lord in a foreign soil?' PS 137:4

Glory be ...

Reflection from Psalm NO 138

The old adage says that; 'well begun is half done.' On the other hand discouragement or sheer lack of energy, may find an undertaking only partially complete. This Psalm provides motivation to finish the task.

UNFINISHED BUSINESS

What a wonderful message for me, Lord:
'The Lord will work out his plans for my life.'
PS 138:8
That you will further all I take in hand,
Complete the work you have begun.

You yourself, Lord, spoke disparagingly
Of those who left unfinished business.
Of the builder who completed only half the tower,
Of the plower who looked back in mid-furrow.

Don't have people say of me,
'He/she began the project but never finished the job.
Bring to a happy conclusion
What you have begun in me.

I am the work of your hands,
Your grace has brought me to where I am.

Lord, you have inspired me to
Start on the road to you,
Give me now the determination
To arrive at my destination!

  'On the day I called, you did answer me,
  My strength of soul you did increase.' PS 138:3

Glory be…

Reflection from Psalm NO 139

God knows all about us, our good points and our failings; yet he cares for us like a loving father.

THE LORD KNOWS ME

Lord, you know me through and through,
You know everything about me.
Every moment you know where I am.
You go in front of me.
You follow me.
You know my past.
You have mapped out my future.
Every day was recorded in your book!

Your knowledge of me sometimes comforts me,
Sometimes frightens me,
But is always beyond my comprehension.

Your care for me is boundless,
You made all parts of my body,
You put them together
In my mother's womb.

In sickness and in health,
In youth and in age,
In happiness and sorrow,
Your limitless power is
Equalled only by your
Infinite goodness and love.

Lord, you know me inside and out.
Now make me know myself!

  'See if there be any wicked way in me,
  And guide me on the way everlasting!' PS 139:24

Glory be …

Reflection from Psalm NO 140

A plea that God will deal justly with those who perpetrate evil, while showing mercy to the hapless victims.

VIOLENCE

Lord, how we long for a world that is truly just!

Every day brings fresh news of some glaring injustice:
Corruption,
Greed, drugs,
New wars broken out,
Shootings,
Bombings,
Even yet, the statistics are rising.

Lord, deliver our nation and world,
From those who resort to violence
To carry out their objectives,
However plausible they may appear.
Heal those who have grown ill
With the madness of war.

While you deal justly, Lord,
With the men and women of violence,
Show mercy too upon the victims
Of their obscene actions.

'Lord, guard me from the hands of the wicked:
From the violent keep me safe.' PS 140:1

Glory be …

Reflection from Psalm NO 141

A prayer of thanks-giving as another day draws to a close. 'When a great moment knocks on the door of your life, its knock is no louder than the beating of your heart, and it is very easy to miss it.'
– BORIS PASTERNAK

LIKE INCENSE

I have called to you, Lord,
Hasten to help me.
Let my prayer rise before you like incense.
The raising of my hands
Like the evening sacrifice.

The day is almost over now, Lord,
I would like to offer it to you,
Such as it is.

I may not have accomplished much,
Yet it rises to you,
Like the last whiffs
From a lighted thurible,
Dissolving into perfume,
Vanishing into the calm around me.

Accept my evening sacrifice, Lord;
Heal my memories,
Gently close the door
On my past,
That I may live in the fullness of the present.

Tomorrow bears on its back,
A satchel, within,
The grace to live that day,
That hour, that moment, for you.

'Let my prayer rise before you like incense,
The raising of my hands like an evening sacrifice.' PS 141:2

Glory be …

Reflection from Psalm NO 142

THE PRISON OF LONELINESS

I cry to the Lord with a loud voice.
I pour out my anguish in his presence,
For I am confused and lost.
You alone know which way I should turn.

I look to the right and see,
There is no one who recognises me.
Every escape is hidden from me,
There is no one who cares for me.
I feel isolated.

Then I prayed to the Lord.
'Lord,' I said,
You heard me before.
You alone can keep me safe.
Hear my cry for I am very low.
Save me from those who would harm me,
They are too strong for me.

Deliver me from the prison of loneliness,
So I can thank you.
My few remaining friends
Will rejoice with me
For all your help.'

  'Bring me out of the prison,
   So that I can thank you.' PS 142:7

Glory be …

Suffering of any kind is mostly a solitary affair. When all is well with us, we have friends and companions to share our prosperity and happiness; but when adversity comes, we are likely to find ourselves nearly, if not entirely, alone.

Reflection from Psalm NO 143

ON A BAD DAY

Lord, must I suffer opposition continually?
Is there no let-up?

I honestly tried to do my best,
But problems confront me all the time.
The list is endless.
I'll spare you the details.

How is it that those who live godly lives
So often suffer?
There must be some recompense
For all our longings and aspirations.

Yet, Lord, it is this hope
Of something far better to come,
That sustains me
Keeps me struggling on.

Come closer, Lord, that I may hear again
Your voice of comfort and concern.

  'Lead me into the land of justice
  For your Spirit is generous.' PS 143:10

Glory be ...

Reflection from Psalm NO 144

Compared to the vastness of God's creation, we humans are but a passing entity. And yet, God can employ us as instruments to affect a lasting impression for good towards the destinies of those whose lives we touch. This Psalm encourages us never to disregard that kind deed or word as being of small significance.

MERELY A BREATH

It is difficult, Lord,
To understand your regard for humankind,
When each of us is
'Merely a breath whose life fades like a shadow.'
PS 144:4

What can be lighter than,
A puff of wind or a passing shadow?
It brings home to me, Lord,
That you are the Reality, the Substance.

Not for me then to right all wrongs,
Solve all the world's problems.
I am but a puff of wind
A passing shadow.

Let my fleeting presence then
Bring a moment of relief
To those whose lives I touch;
A gesture of good will
In a world that is laden with sorrow.

'Bid heaven stoop, Lord, and come down to earth
With your touch … reach down from heaven and save me.' PS 144:5

Glory be …

Reflection from Psalm NO 145

We owe a great debt to the dedicated faithfulness of past generations who have passed on the torch of faith. The good people do, should never be 'interred with their bones.'

THE GENERATION LINK

I will praise you, my God and King.
I will bless your name each day and forever.
Let every passing generation teach its children,
Let them hand on in story,
The mighty deeds of the Lord.

While praying, Lord, I recall the past,
My own history and that of my people.
How gracious and merciful you are,
Slow to anger and full of kindness.
You open your generous hands,
And satisfy the desire of every living thing.

Each generation instructs the other,
Handing on beliefs and practices
An unbroken chain of memories,
A chorus of unity
In a world of discord.

They will talk about the greatness of your kingdom.
A kingdom that never ends.
For the Lord rules over every generation.

'Each age will praise your deeds to the next,
And shall proclaim your mighty works.' PS 145:4

Glory be …

Reflection from Psalm NO 146

PLACE NOT YOUR TRUST ...

Place not your trust in flattery, or
Your dependence on the approval of others.
Trust rather in the Lord, who alone
Judges the human heart.

Do not put your trust in rulers,
In human beings, who cannot save.
They pass on quickly,
Their greatest leaders fail.

The Lord is everlasting.
His designs full of wisdom.
He is true to his pledged word.
What he says, he does.

The Lord gives justice to the poor.
He provides nourishment for the hungry.
He brings release to the prisoner.
He befriends the innocent.
He comforts the burdened.
He opens the eyes of the blind.
He watches over people visiting our land.

'The Lord will reign for all time ... praise the Lord!' PS 146:10

Glory be ...

Reflection from Psalm NO 147A

DEPENDENCE

Our great God knows the number of stars,
He calls each orbit by name.
The same Lord it is who heals the
Broken hearted and binds up their wounds.

His greatness is matched
Only by his tenderness,
While his strength parallels his mercy.

The Lord appoints the times and seasons.
He covers the sky with rain-clouds.
He refreshes the earth
With water for its fruits.

He is the harvester of all living things.
He supplies provisions for all his creatures.

Such is God's loving care and providence for all creation.
Well merited the praise and gratitude of
His children who understand
Their dependence on him.

Call me by my name, Lord,
As you call the stars in heaven.
And one day, use my name to call me
To your side forever.

'The Lord sets the number of stars,
Gives to all of them their names.' PS 147:4

Glory be…

Reflection from Psalm NO 147B

WINTER

I woke up this morning, Lord.
I looked out my window.
The earth had turned to white.
You have spread a pall of snow
In all its brilliance.
You have covered the countryside
The valleys,
The mountains,
The city;
All mantled by the invisible hand
Of the Master Artist,
During the silent night.

Your care covers all, Lord,
The saints and sinners,
The rich and poor,
The wise and simple.

Clothe with your blessings and your grace
My faltering ways.
Send out your word
To melt the ice of my heart.

   'The Lord spreads snow like wool,
   And scatters hoarfrost like ashes.' PS 147:16

Glory be …

Reflection from Psalms NOS 148, 149, 150

When the composer Gustav Mahler first saw the Niagra Falls, he exclaimed: 'Crescendo!' Similarly in this, the final Psalms of the Psalter, we have a grand finale of praise and thanksgiving.

PRAISE THE LORD!

Praise the Lord, O heavens!
Praise him from the skies!
Praise him, sun and moon,
And all you twinkling stars.
Let everything he has made
Give praise to him.

Praise him down here on this planet.
Let the rulers and all the people
Give him praise.
His glory is greater than
All of earth and heaven.

Sing the Lord a new song.
Acclaim his name with dancing.
Praise his name with the trumpet
With oboe, strings and harp.

Let everything that breathes
Give praise to the Lord!

   'You, too, praise him!
   Praise the Lord!' PS 150:6

Glory be …

Envoi

When the Paraclete comes,
whom I shall send to you from the Father,
the Spirit of truth who issues from the Father,
he will be my witness.
And you too will be witnesses,
because you have been with me from the beginning.
JOHN 15:26-7

Index of Subjects

The number(s) of the psalms are given after the subject. Sometimes a number of psalms refer to the same subject.